Keats's Odes

Keats's Odes
A Lover's Discourse
Anahid Nersessian

The University of Chicago Press · *Chicago and London*

The University of Chicago Press, Chicago 60637
The University of Chicago Press, Ltd., London
© 2021 by The University of Chicago
All rights reserved. No part of this book may be used or reproduced
in any manner whatsoever without written permission, except in
the case of brief quotations in critical articles and reviews. For more
information, contact the University of Chicago Press, 1427 E. 60th
St., Chicago, IL 60637.
Published 2021
Paperback edition 2023
Printed in the United States of America

32 31 30 29 28 27 26 25 24 23   1 2 3 4 5

ISBN-13: 978-0-226-76267-8 (cloth)
ISBN-13: 978-0-226-82652-3 (paper)
ISBN-13: 978-0-226-76270-8 (e-book)
DOI: https://doi.org/10.7208/chicago/9780226762708.001.0001

Library of Congress Cataloging-in-Publication Data

Names: Nersessian, Anahid, 1982- author.
Title: Keats's odes : a lover's discourse / Anahid Nersessian.
Description: Chicago ; London : The University of Chicago Press,
    2021. | Includes bibliographical references and index.
Identifiers: LCCN 2020028776 | ISBN 9780226762678 (cloth) |
    ISBN 9780226762708 (ebook)
Subjects: LCSH: Keats, John, 1795-1821—Criticism and interpretation. |
    English poetry—19th century—History and criticism.
Classification: LCC PR4837 .N37 2021 | DDC 821/.7—dc23
LC record available at https://lccn.loc.gov/2020028776

♾ This paper meets the requirements of ANSI/NISO Z39.48-1992
(Permanence of Paper).

For Tatianna, who told me to write it

Contents

The heart uselessly opens
To 3 words, which is too little

George Oppen

Preface

If you've never read anything on Keats's odes before, this book should not be your first stop. It is a collection of essays based on intimate, often idiosyncratic responses to the poems. In fact it is probably better to call them meditations instead of essays. The literary critics who've taught me the most about Keats are rarely if ever cited in what follows, as this is a book designed for non-specialists. For those who would like to read further, I recommend starting with Walter Jackson Bate, *The Stylistic Development of Keats*; James Chandler, chapter 7 of *England in 1819: The Politics of Literary Culture and the Case of Romantic Historicism*; Paul H. Fry, "History, Existence, and 'To Autumn'"; Marjorie Levinson, *Keats's Life of Allegory*; Jerome J. McGann, *The Romantic Ideology: A Critical Investigation*; Christopher Ricks, *Keats and Embarrassment*: Nicholas Roe, *John Keats and the Culture of Dissent*, plus Roe's excellent biography; Helen Vendler, *The Odes of John Keats*; and Susan Wolfson, *Formal Charges: The Shaping of Poetry in British Romanticism* along with various essays.

While I was writing, Jonathan Kramnick pointed me toward Dorothy Van Ghent's unfinished *Keats: The Myth of the Hero*, edited and revised by Jeffrey Cane Robinson. It is out of print but well worth tracking down. The best biography is probably Bate's *John Keats*, but Aileen Ward's *John Keats: The Making of the Poet* is my favorite. As the book makes clear, I think any serious appreciation of Keats's poetry begins with the section on "Private Property and Communism" from Karl Marx's *Economic and Philosophical Manuscripts of 1844* and the first volume of *Capital*, too.

Introduction

John Keats was born on October 31, 1795, and he died of tuberculosis on February 23, 1821, aged twenty-five. In that narrow patch of existence he composed some of the most unrepentingly alive poems in the English language. It is possible that, had he survived, he would have written no more; quitting had always been an option, and he needed real money to support himself and his fiancée, Fanny Brawne. It is also possible that he would have kept writing, and possible too that he would have burrowed even deeper into the broken heart of his century, which, he knew, was reordering time and space in answer to the demands of a new and rapacious economic system. George Bernard Shaw saw in Keats the makings of "a full-blooded modern revolutionist," and if he didn't reach the barricades he did belong on them, because there was nothing Keats loved more than us: those who know this is not all we are meant to be. His poetry is a record of that love and its wild, inconvenient expression. It is a lover's discourse, at once compassionate, exacting, indecent, and pure.

This book collects six of Keats's poems, known together as the Great Odes. I follow each ode with a short essay that is both critical and autobiographical, although the autobiographical dimension will not always be obvious. In that sense, the essays work like the odes. Odes, roughly speaking, are poems meant to celebrate something or someone, but because they are written from a place of emotional excess or ferment it's easy for them to tip over into more private preoccupations: thus Percy Bysshe Shelley's "Ode to the West Wind," which connects the cycle of the seasons to the here today, gone tomorrow movement of revolutionary struggle, also erupts into the furiously personal cri de coeur "I fall upon the thorns of life—I bleed!" In writing about Keats's odes, I have tried to prop myself open to this same uneven traffic of literary and intimate concerns. This book, then, is a love story: between me and Keats, and not just Keats.

Keats himself was famously lovable, despite having been born (he said) into an "unpromising morning." That sense of bleakness, of having failed before he had begun, dogged him. He was poor. He was short, six inches below average, and in ill health. Once he began publishing his work was almost universally panned. He was temperamental, obsessive, and thin-skinned, and his childhood, which was traumatic, left him "nervous, morbid," in the words of his brother George. All the same, he amassed a small army of devoted friends, one of whom called him "the most lovable associate ... 'that ever lived in the tide of times.'" Of his death, or perhaps their relationship, Brawne wrote, "I have not got over it, and never shall."

When I say this book is a love story, I mean it is about things that cannot be gotten over—like this world, and some of the people in it.

*

The word that gets used most often in conjunction with Keats is *sensuous*. He is fascinated by how things feel, and by the capacity of metaphor to register the dizzying strangeness of being a body among others. Only Keats could come up with "the thrilling liquidity of dewy piping" or "a breathless honey-feel of bliss," and not always to his credit. The early poetry, like the soupy epic *Endymion*, expels an unfortunate phrase every couple of lines: "well-wooing sun," "night-swollen mushrooms," "fire-tailed exhalations," and so on. This kind of writing disgusted contemporary reviewers, who called it "puerile" and "effeminate," "unhealthy" and "unclean"; "In Wordsworth," one sniffed, "there is no such unhealthy lusciousness." Lord Byron agreed: "Such poetry," he declared, "is a sort of mental masturbation," and elsewhere he snickers about "Johnny Keats's piss-a-bed-poetry." A century later William Butler Yeats slides into the same vein:

> I see a schoolboy when I think of him
> With face and nose pressed to a sweet-shop window,
> For certainly he sank into his grave
> His senses and his heart unsatisfied,
> And made—being poor, ailing and ignorant,
> Shut out from all the luxury of the world,
> The coarse-bred son of a livery stable-keeper—
> Luxuriant song.

Yeats makes explicit what Byron doesn't have to: not only is Keats's poetry sexually deviant, its indecency (or "luxuriance") is amplified by his lower-middle-class status. The Romantic period had a taste for so-called peasant poets like Stephen Duck, Ann Yearsley, and John Clare, but Keats was not a peasant. Worse, he skimmed the proletarian perimeter while being *aspirationally* "shabby-genteel," "a fanciful dreaming tea-drinker" with a false claim on respectability. In the alchemy of nineteenth-century social prejudice, this rendered him at once oversexed and insufficiently masculine. He was an outcast and a striver and out of genital control, "f–gg–g his Imagination" (Byron again) instead of a nice warm body. It's a singularly nasty assessment, and it sticks.

It sticks, in part, because when he died, Keats's friends played up elements of this picture, and the Victorian era (which Keats missed by just nine years) ate it up. He was a special favorite of the Pre-Raphaelites, who mined his work for inspiration; in their poems and canvases, colorless young men repine in the arms of no-good women with hair like candy floss. He became then what he still is to many people now: an escapist, rolling around in visions of fairies and butterflies, deliriously aroused but somehow still chaste. In the big-box bookstores of my youth, you could always find cheap editions of his poems, squat volumes with gold paint sprayed along their edges. The checkout line held stacks of blank notebooks with Frank Dicksee's 1901 painting *La Belle Dame sans Merci* spilled across the front and Keats's more notable quotables— "I am certain of nothing but of the holiness of the heart's affections and the truth of the imagination"—printed in the margins. The poetry, it seemed, was safe, commercial, decorative. Above all, it was apolitical.

This would have stuck painfully in Keats's craw. The reason he got so much negative attention in the press is because he hung out with well-known radicals, and was a radical himself. When one reviewer dubbed Keats and his friends "the Cockney School of Poetry," he didn't just mean that they were, as the Brits say, N.O.C.D. (*not our class, dear*), he meant they were left-wingers, even revolutionaries. This is a view of Keats most academics now share, thanks in large measure to the legendary Walter Jackson Bate—who went from busing tables in campus dining halls to Harvard professor—whose 1963 biography turned Yeats's picture of the schoolboy randy for candy on its head. Bate's Keats was a bruiser, his Jacobin sympathies hung in plain sight. Today, if you suggest to a room full of Keats scholars that their man is apolitical, you might be asked to step outside.

The trouble with this view of Keats is that it rests heavily on his biography and not much, if at all, on his poetry. Although that poetry was written in dark times—in the aftermath of the Napoleonic Wars and in the middle of the catastrophic economic downtown they engendered; during the breakneck acceleration of the Industrial Revolution, with its unspeakable dependence on human slavery in the Caribbean and elsewhere; in the wake of the Peterloo Massacre, when armed cavalry maimed or killed a still-unknown number of peaceful protestors—it says close to nothing about them. Keats's radicalism lies elsewhere, in his style.

It is true that Keats is a sensualist, that he is obsessed with capturing the heady particularities of taste and touch. It is also true that these tendencies can make his work seem anti-intellectual and even immoral—a gaudy retreat from the world's horrors. He did once claim that "with a great Poet the sense of Beauty overcomes every other consideration, or rather obliterates all consideration" and, according to his friend Benjamin Robert Haydon, "once covered his tongue and throat as far as he could reach with Cayenne pepper, in order to appreciate the delicious coldness of claret in all its glory." In 1880, Matthew Arnold raised these points by way of complaining about Keats's "sensuous strain," and also by way of complaining about his fans, "admirers whose pawing and fondness does not good but harm to the fame of Keats" by concentrating "attention upon what in him is least wholesome and most questionable." He is thinking of lines like these:

Light feet, dark violet eyes, and parted hair;
  Soft dimpled hands, white neck, and creamy breast,

Are things on which the dazzled senses rest
Till the fond, fixed eyes forget they stare.

Arnold was more right than he knew. Keats's senses always strain, are always under stress. *Dazzled* does not just mean impressed but stricken, brought low, obliterated by beauty as by a blow to the head; it chimes with both *fond* and *fixed*, since the former means loving to the point of stupidity and the latter sounds a syllable out of "crucifixion." This is desire as duress, embodiment as ordeal.

The person who's really onto him is Shaw, who makes the surprising suggestion that passages of Keats would not be out of place in *Das Kapital* and that Karl Marx, had he written poetry, would have written it like Keats.[1] In *Isabella; or, the Pot of Basil*, Keats anticipates Marx's claim that industrial production requires an especially brutal "expenditure of human brain, nerves, muscles, and sense organs," and the poem, much like *Das Kapital*, is downright ghoulish (the action revolves around a severed head). Keats's poetry is chock full of viscera, and if his grislier images owe much to his stint as a medical student, they are also signs that Keats grasps something deep about capital's cannibal logic. For every set of soft dimpled hands, there are weary ones that "swelt / In torched mines and noisy factories," and for every creamy breast, "many once proud-quiver'd loins ... melt[ing] / In blood from stinging whip."

Early on Marx decided that "the forming of the five senses is a labour of the entire history of the world down to the present." Any attempt to understand the way things are had to be rigorously carnal: it could not operate "solely within the orbit of thought ... devoid of eyes, of teeth, of ears, of everything." Note the allusion to Jaques's "All the world's a stage" speech in

(1) In his youth Marx did write poetry, though it reads more like his beloved Shelley.

As You Like It, where old age is the state of being "Sans teeth, sans eyes, sans taste, sans everything." Keats had the same idea. His poetry concentrates on the effortful, even agonizing work of shaping the body's response to the world. He loved the lines from Shakespeare's *Venus and Adonis* that describe the goddess recoiling from the sight of her dead lover like a snail "whose tender horns being hit, / Shrinks backwards in his shelly cave with pain," eventually drafting them to describe the "innumerable compositions and decompositions which take place between the intellect and its thousand materials before it arrives at that trembling delicate and snail-horn perception of Beauty." To perceive is to hurt—sometimes a little, sometimes a lot. If the task of Marx's critique of political economy is to locate the cause of that pain, the task of Keats's poetry is to make it unforgettable.

The best poets, Keats says, are "camelion": they change to match their surroundings, sometimes entering fully into the psychic and sensational orbit of other beings. Keats gave this talent a name: it was Negative Capability, and he had it to spare. "When I am in a room with people," he confided, "the identity of every one in the room begins to press upon me, so that I am in a very little time annihilated—not only among men; it would be the same in a nursery of Children."

This is empathy of an especially extravagant kind: it involves "filling some other body," to the point of knowing everything about how it thinks, feels, moves, and affects the bodies around it. In *The Eve of St. Agnes,* a girl getting ready for bed "unclasps her warmed jewels one by one," the offhand adjective *warmed* cradling a remnant of her blood's own heat; the sonnet "To Mrs. Reynolds's Cat" describes a "gentle mew" as "upraise[d]," lifted through the air from the floor. It's a poetics of the 360° view and the fourth dimension. It makes language thick and extends its reach through time, until it becomes capable of preserving what William Blake calls "every little act" of existence—kinetic exchange and thermal transfer, stimulus and response—in an undaunted assertion that, even amid the waste and savagery of history, "not one sigh, nor smile, nor tear, / One hair, nor particle of dust, not one can pass away."

Love makes a good subject for this kind of writing. For one thing, it is a paradigmatic case of Negative Capability. "You have absorb'd me," Keats wrote to Brawne, "I have a sensation at the present moment as though I was dissolving." For another, it is as good a name as any for the wish not to lose what the conditions of our lives demand be lost to us. You could call that our humanity if, like Marx, you were willing to define "human nature" as "communal nature." You could call it freedom if, like Keats, you were willing to define freedom as vulnerability, an absolute openness to the annihilation of self. When Keats writes about love, which is almost all the time, he offers it to us in exactly this light, as the feeling of knowing, for once, what we are truly capable of—the widening circle of pleasure and joy, the depth of a loss that is also a gift and relic, unable to pass away.

The Great Odes record love's complementary processes of absorption and dissolution. They are, in Keats's phrase, "havens of intenseness" where the most unsparing expressions of desire can be at once sheltered and laid bare. Sexually engrossed though never explicit, they make intimacy into a form of endurance, difficult but necessary. This is an erotic sublime in which, as Keats says, we are *pressed upon* by those to whom we come close, and those to whom we never seem to get close enough. Again and again, trials of longing, needing, having, caring, giving in, breaking down, leaving and failing to leave behind are met with candor and a fearless enthusiasm, for this poetry is honest—not in any limited moral sense, but because it is obstinate in its commitment to loving without shame or reservation. An ode by Keats is just that: an anchorage for big feelings that, in their sheer ungovernability, test what it might be like to be really free. It's an imperfect approximation, to be sure. Poetry is the art of taking what you can get.

*

Keats was, as Yeats says, the son of a stable-keeper. He left school at fifteen to train as an apothecary, and earned his license—which allowed him to work as a pharmacist, physician, and surgeon—in 1816. When he gave up medicine for poetry, it was much to the surprise of his childhood friends, who remembered him as *not literary.* "His penchant," one testified, "was for fighting":

> He would fight any one—morning, noon, and night, his brother among the rest. It was meat and drink to him.... His sensibility was as remarkable as his indifference to be thought well of by the master as a 'good boy' and to his tasks in general.... He was in every way the creature of passion.... The generosity and daring of his character with the extreme beauty and animation of his face made I remember an impression on me—and being some years his junior I was obliged to woo his friendship—in which I succeeded, but not till I had fought several battles. This violence and vehemence—this pugnacity and generosity of disposition—in passions of tears or outrageous fits of laughter—always in extremes—will help to paint Keats in his boyhood. Associated as they were with an extraordinary beauty of person and expression, these qualities captivated the boys, and no one was more popular.

For Bate and Keats's other, almost exclusively male biographers, these testaments of physical bravado and sterling conscience—he once knocked the sauce out of an older boy he found torturing a kitten—prove that Keats was a healthy, red-blooded kid. They prove, in other words, that he was not the sissy Byron and the Victorians made him out to be. I could go on at length about the gender politics couched in these nervous assertions that Keats really was one of the guys, but there's something else that bothers me, too. I know it's a modern, not at all nineteenth-century thought, and yet I wonder: Did anyone ever take aside this little boy, *always in extremes*, and ask, "is something going on at home?"

In fact there was. When Keats was eight, his father was killed in a riding accident; his mother, née Frances Jennings, remarried almost instantly, and then she disappeared. When she returned five years later, she was dying. Although the source is suspect—he is Richard Abbey, guardian of the Keats children and a character right out of Dickens—Keats's mother was evidently "addicted to drinking," her alcoholism "a temporary Gratification to those inordinate Appetites which seem to have been in one stage or another constantly soliciting her." You will hear the echoes of Byron's critique: mother and son, immoderate in appetite, degraded by pleasure, solicited and soliciting. "Her passions were so ardent," Abbey sniped, "it was dangerous to be alone with her."

"It's true what they say," writes Rivka Galchen, "that a baby gives you reason to live. But also, a baby is a reason that it is not permissible to die. There are days when this does not feel good." Frances Jennings didn't know she wasn't allowed to die, or it was a responsibility that choked her. As a young woman, she liked how she looked; when the streets were muddy, she would lift her skirts high to show off her legs. In eight years she gave birth to five children, one of whom died in infancy. John, her oldest, did not like her to leave the house; he had a dependent's instinct to get between Frances and herself and thus to save his own life, too. Haydon reports that "at 5 years of age or there abouts, he got hold of a naked sword . . . His mother wanted to go out, but he threatened her so furiously that she burst into tears." When she came home to die, Keats, now fourteen, "sat up whole nights [with her] in a great chair, would suffer nobody to give her medicine but himself, or even cook her food." At school, he "gave way to such impassioned and prolonged grief (hiding himself in a nook under the master's desk) as awakened the liveliest pity and sympathy in all who saw him."

Keats would eventually stop fighting, but he remained on the hunt for nooks where impassioned and prolonged feelings of all kinds could linger and intensify, private worlds that are not really private and whose borders bleed out. Some of these worlds became poems, and some of them became the letters he would write to Brawne. These are often praised as some of the best love letters ever written, and they are. They can also be paranoid, swinging from helpless infatuation—"I never knew before, what such a love as you have made me feel, was; I did not believe in it; my Fancy was afraid of it, lest it should burn me up"—to dictatorial command: "If you could really what is call'd enjoy yourself at a Party—if you can smile in peoples faces, and wish them to admire you now, you never have nor ever will love me—I see life in nothing but the ce[r]tainty of your Love—convince me of it my sweetest. If I am not somehow convinc'd I shall die of agony." It doesn't take a great leap of psychoanalytic faith to imagine where this insecurity came from, nor why it so often discharged itself in runaway-train fantasies where the only possible termination of love is death. "You must be mine," he told Brawne, "to die upon the rack if I want you."

I tell these stories about Keats not to put him on the couch, and anyway he was his own most relentless self-excavator.

He worried that he didn't have "a right feeling toward women," and was disappointed in himself for struggling to square the reality that they were his "equal[s]" with the illusion that they were all goddesses, "ethereal above men." I tell these stories about Keats because they helped me love him, since it is hard not to love other people's damage, or at least it has been hard for me.

*

In the thick of a colossal heartbreak or else teetering on the lip of one, I went to see a witch. Someone had brandished forgiveness in front of me like baby Keats's sword, and I wanted to know how to answer. The question, I could tell, bored her. Frankly it bored me, and we had bigger fish to fry. One of the first things she said was, "you spend a lot of time with dead people."

I had never thought of it that way, but she's exactly right. I told her that, yes, I think about dead people all day. I read what they've written and try to understand what they've meant; then I stand in front of teenagers and offer up intimate details about their lives—their exercise routines and puerperal fevers, the children and ideals they tried to hold onto and those they cast aside. I explain how close they came to imagining communism, mostly as an excuse to drill into my students what communism is (*"the land belongs to no one"* and *"the fruits belong to all"*—Sylvain Maréchal, 1796). If I'm being completely honest, I do feel sometimes that they are in the room with me, and I tell the witch that lately one of them has a presence that feels very angry, as if he has taken a side in the matter of the heartbreak, and it is not mine. The witch is skeptical. "I don't know what to tell you about that," she says, "but you need to be more careful with spirits."

Keats, too, spent a lot of time with dead people, as a medical student dissecting cadavers and, like me, in his head. He had a feeling he was being watched—by Shakespeare. To Haydon he copped to having "notions of a good Genius presiding over" him, then asked, with his usual blend of diffidence and bravado, "Is it too Daring to Fancy Shakespeare this Presider?" If I've had similar notions of Keats, I have no idea why he might preside over me. I've never had literary ambitions. In college the only people who called themselves poets were wealthy, freckled New Englanders who dressed as puns for Halloween. I threw in my lot with the art majors, soft-spoken lefties, and kids in bands, was stoned all day and spent weekend mornings in a friend's attic room, where we tried to wrap our heads around Althusser and Fanon. There was a group of us who identified, though we'd never say so out loud, as critics: people who know what words mean. To this day I don't like being called a writer, even in the indirect context of a compliment like "You're a good writer." I don't like the compliment either; in grad school I learned that *good writer* was a synonym for *con artist*.

If Keats is presiding over me, I guess he has his reasons; he's been doing it for a long time. One day, when I must have been around eleven, I pulled a book called *Love's Aspects* down from my parents' shelf. Edited by Jean Garrigue, it promised to be a collection of the world's great love poems, but inside were also Keats's letters to Brawne—not poems at all but, in their naked sense of direction, irreducibly epistolary documents. Once I learned what happened to these two young people, I felt personally cheated by the tragedy. I wanted more of them both, including or maybe especially Brawne, whose voice is almost absent from the historical record. I promptly read all the Keats I could, including the great mid-century biographies—by Aileen Ward, Robert Gittings, Bate—and from here it was an easy glide to Shelley, Byron, Coleridge, even Wordsworth, the awful man who had insulted Keats at a dinner party by calling *Endymion* "a very pretty piece of Paganism."

It's hard to overstate what a lifeline this literature, which I didn't yet know to call the Western canon, was for me, or how unambivalent about it I was. My father was born and raised in Tehran, and my mother, whose family is Welsh, in a depressed former mining town that used to be called Lake City, Tennessee, site of the Coal Creek War and a stone's throw from the Fraterville Mine Disaster. Eastern Armenian, with its chic cargo of loan words from Farsi and French, was the first language I spoke and the whole of my identity—with a name as conspicuous as mine, I didn't have much choice—but in the 1980s and '90s, spun on a loop of hostage crises, arms deals, burning flags and burning oil fields, commercial airplanes shot out of the sky, it was the Iranian bit that caused the most trouble.

Like many kids who don't look like their classmates, who cart around odd names and are told, loudly and sternly, by the teacher that when they choose construction paper on which to draw a self-portrait they had better not choose white, since anyone can see their skin is much darker than that, I figured out early that WASPs couldn't be trusted with their own culture. I aligned myself with the literary past not to be like them but as a higher order of civilization, a bulwark against the barbarian hordes of saddle-shoe blondes who didn't know the difference between Iran and Iraq but took the Gulf War as their latest provocation to kick me literally in the teeth. Besides, being "good at it" was praised and rewarded. When I got in trouble, which was often, it was the English teachers who had my back.

Among the dead, I was anonymous and nearly blank, a disembodied competence. That felt good, was a relief, and as I read more, got smarter and more skilled, I began to hope that the past might need me as much as I needed it. It wasn't until later that a certain disharmony began creeping into my alliance with my books. I don't mean the propitious analytic friction that discovering feminism and, around the same time, Marxism generated between us. I mean the smaller, sadder recognition that this literature could not imagine me—that if it had helped give me a place in the world there was still no place for me in it. Even "my blankness," as Renee Gladman says, had no shape there, and yet it seemed there was no place else it could have been born: "When I looked for it—reaching into myself for it—it was only the page that I found. I didn't know whether at some point in my past, perhaps at the very first moment I set out to write, the page had fallen out of me or I had risen out of it."

What I mean is this. As far as the past is concerned, we exceptionally modern people—the immigrant, the feminist, the communist, the differently desiring—will always be unsubstantiated, a possibility no one thought to put a frame around. By contrast there are those in possession of identities, or aspects of identities, that guarantee they will always be included in the tiny circle Wordsworth draws when he defines the poet as "a man speaking to men," even if they would rather not be. You could describe this state of being unimaginable as a kind of unrequited love but even that implies a relationship, or at least a relation. What I have in mind is a more absolute sense of not mattering.

I love Keats not because I belong in his poetry, but because his poetry wants so much to belong to us—to those who know intimately why a relentless self-exposure to the world has to be made, somehow, into a virtue because otherwise it is just abuse. I use the word *virtue* without irony; it could be replaced with *tactic*. To say that his poetry is a lover's discourse is to acknowledge that, in love, the line between a strength and a liability can be hard to determine. The dream of Marx's communism is that the basic agony of having a body might be expropriated or stolen away from all unnecessary and debilitating uses of human life and remade into the condition of shared freedom. Keats is not far off, and when he told Brawne that "all my unhappiest days and nights have I find not at all cured me of my love of Beauty, but made it so intense that I am miserable when you are not with me," he didn't just mean Brawne but, I believe, the very chance of other people: their dream, their freedom. He took his own history of not mattering and turned it into a poetry that voids all the lethal systems and prejudices that decide who lives and who dies, and he did it by insisting that what we love is sacred, as is the act of loving it. He may not have been speaking to me but this, in Sean Bonney's ineradicable words, is what I've heard: "for 'love / of beauty' say fuck the police."

*

"The distinguishing character of an ode," according to one eighteenth-century commentator, "is sweetness." Really it's sweetness in the sense of sweet talk: ulterior and quietly demanding. Because odes are poems of praise or commemoration, they typically talk to or at something or someone. This is why odes so often make use of a rhetorical device called apostrophe, an address to an entity who won't or cannot answer back: the wind, a corpse, a concept, a god. Not coincidentally, Roland Barthes, in his *Fragments d'un Discours Amoureux*—translated as *A Lover's Discourse*—suggests that love is marked by a strange compulsion to speak to those who aren't there. This is a "preposterous situation": "You have gone (which I lament), you are here (since I am addressing you.)"

For Barthes, this apostrophic "discourse of absence" is

a version of what Freud describes as the game of fort/da, in which the child faced with his mother leaving for work uses a toy to control his anxiety, throwing it away from him and then pulling it close in imitation of the absolute authority he wants over his parent, and in which the adult falls dysfunctionally back on a grown-up version of the same strategy, using not a toy but the discredited person herself: "All right, then, go away! I don't need you," and so forth, in Freud's ventriloquism. But if love is an invitation to act out—to drift into habits of ambivalent attachment left over from childhood—it is also an invitation to refine language ad infinitum. "Absence persists," and if we have to endure it we might as well "*manipulate* it: transform the distortion of time into an oscillation, produce rhythm," delaying "as long as possible the moment when the other might topple sharply from absence into death," might cross the line between *not there now* and *never here again*.

Part of what makes *A Lover's Discourse* so compelling is the way each of its chapters focuses on a single word from love's vocabulary, polishing and proliferating its meaning in an effort to defer the inevitable. From that single word, the entire history of a relationship unspools only to be wound back up again, circling the memory of an experience at once utterly specific and humblingly universal. Regardless of whom you last loved, or when, or for how long, we've all been using the same pocket dictionary:

> Every contact, for the lover, raises the question of an answer: the skin is asked to reply.... A squeeze of the hand—enormous documentation—a tiny gesture within the palm, a knee which doesn't move away, an arm extended, as if quite naturally, along the back of a sofa and against which the other's head gradually comes to rest—this is the paradisiac realm of subtle

and clandestine signs: a kind of festival not of the senses but of meaning.

As Barthes makes clear, you do not need another person to help you interpret these signs, least of all the person you love. They are best studied in isolation, and that too is the condition of the ode which, like any lyric poem, understands solitude as the prerequisite for entertaining a problem.

The problem, in Barthes's phrasing, is this: "not . . . *make it stop!* but: *I want to understand* (what is happening to me)!" Each of Keats's odes plumbs states of feeling that accompany the drama of this inquiry. In terms of their structure, they are all more or less modified (Keats said "better") sonnets, rearrangements and dilations of the fourteen-line form. His models were Petrarch and Shakespeare, but ultimately he decided that Italian sonnets worked only in Italian and that the English variant, with its tidy final couplet, was too poised and self-assured. By contrast, the stanzas Keats invented for his odes are messy and meandering, their rhymes often partial and often forgettable. They describe the soul's encounter with something hard—a thought, an event, a feeling, a pleasure or an undiluted pain—and that process of description is slow, difficult, erratic. It is also open-ended. The odes are love poems: it is hard to tell when they're over.

Somebody once told me *love* is the best word to write but also the hardest. Keats uses it all the time, with a kind of originary fervor like he's Adam naming the animals: this is love, and this is love, and this too, this is also love. I'm more of a stickler, so it's hard for me to say what I must, that I wrote to understand what was happening to me, and I couldn't get to the end of it. Although this book is not a memoir but a work of literary criticism, the whole of a particular love is folded inside it.

The first and last essays in the book are fairly conventional pieces of scholarship, while the second, on "Ode on a Grecian Urn," introduces an autobiographical element to help consider the poem in light of recent debates around the political function of the Western literary canon. The three essays in the middle, on the three least famous odes, tell a story—indirectly, in fits and starts, through words I borrowed when I couldn't use my own. It is, as I've said, a love story, but like everything else in this book it is also about the forming of the five senses in this place, at this time, about what is happening to us now that we have collectively reached yet another set of prospects to call unendurable. For me, these stories will always belong to each other, and maybe that's what Dorothy Van Ghent had in mind when, in a discarded draft of a never-finished book on Keats, she admits that Keats's poems were "somehow entangled with my own psychic processes,

> disorders, discontents, fleeting fantasies and promises, "ideals" crippled in the course of life and swallowed by the unconscious because they didn't seem to work in the pressing actualities of existence, were in fact a hindrance and a source of anxiety in meeting economic problems and all those difficulties which make it so doubtful whether one shall sink or swim. Apparently Keats's poems represented buried elements of myself, killed off by the terrible rigors of existence, and insistently hammering for recognition, showing that they were still there. I had a notion that there lay in this phenomenon a general description of the "serious meaning" of poetry[.]

When he was dying, Keats said of Brawne, "I see her as a figure eternally vanishing." These words are for the love I still see that way, and for the love that is still here, and ours.

Sources

Roland Barthes. *A Lover's Discourse: Fragments*. Translated by Richard Howard. New York: Hill and Wang, 2001.

Walter Jackson Bate. *John Keats*. Cambridge, MA: Harvard University Press, 1963.

William Blake. *Jerusalem; or, The Emanation of the Giant Albion*. In *The Complete Poetry and Prose of William Blake*, edited by David V. Erdman. Rev. ed. New York: Anchor Books, 1982.

Sean Bonney. "Corpus Hermeticum: On the Revolutions of the Heavenly Spheres." In *Letters Against the Firmament*. London: Enitharmon Press, 2015.

Frances "Fanny" Brawne. Letter to Frances "Fanny" Keats, dated 23 May 1821. In *The Letters of Fanny Brawne to Fanny Keats, 1820–1824*. New York: Oxford University Press, 1937.

George Gordon, Lord Byron. Letters to John Murray, dated 12 October 1820, and 20 November 1820. In *Byron's Letters and Journals*, vol. 7, edited by Leslie A. Marchand. 12 vols. Cambridge, MA: Harvard University Press, 1973-81.

Temple Henry Croker, Thomas Williams, and Samuel Clark. *The Complete Dictionary of Arts and Sciences, in which the Whole Circle of Human Learning is explained, and the Difficulties attending the Acquisition of Every Art, whether Liberal or Mechanical, are removed, in the most easy and familiar Manner*. 2 vols. London: Printed for the authors, 1765.

Sigmund Freud. *Beyond the Pleasure Principle*. Edited and translated by James Strachey. New York: W. W. Norton, 1990.

Rivka Galchen. *Little Labors*. New York: New Directions, 2016.

Renee Gladman. *Calamities*. Seattle: Wave Books, 2016.

John Keats. *Endymion, a Poetic Romance*. In *Complete Poems*, edited by Jack Stillinger. Cambridge, MA: Harvard University Press, 1982.

———. *Isabella; or, the Pot of Basil*. In Stillinger, *Complete Poems*.

———. "To Mrs. Reynolds's Cat." In Stillinger, *Complete Poems*.

———. "Woman! when I behold thee, flippant, vain." In Stillinger, *Complete Poems*.

———. Letter to Benjamin Bailey, dated 22 November 1817. In *The Letters of John Keats.*, vol. 1, edited by Hyder Edward Rollins. 2 vols. Cambridge, MA: Harvard University Press, 1958.

———. Letter to Bailey, dated 18 July 1818. In Rollins, *Letters of John Keats*, vol. 1.

———. Letter to Fanny Brawne, dated 13 October 1819. In Rollins, *Letters of John Keats*, vol. 1.

———. Letter to Brawne, dated May 1820. In Rollins, *Letters of John Keats*, vol. 1.

———. Letter to Benjamin Robert Haydon, dated 10 May 1817. In Rollins, *Letters of John Keats*, vol. 1.

———. Letter to Haydon, dated 8 April 1818. In Rollins, *Letters of John Keats*, vol. 1.

Sylvain Maréchal. *Manifesto of the Equals*. Translated by Mitchell Abidor. https://www.marxists.org/history/france/revolution/conspiracy-equals/1796/manifesto.htm.

Karl Marx. [Private Property and Communism. Various Stages of Development of Communist Views. Crude, Equalitarian Communism and Communism as Socialism Coinciding with Humaneness]. In *Economic and Philosophic Manuscripts of 1844*, translated by Martin Milligan. Amherst, NY: Prometheus Books, 1988.

———. *Capital.* Vol. 1. Translated by Ben Fowkes. London: Penguin, 1990.

William Shakespeare. *As You Like It*. In *The Oxford Shakespeare*, edited by Stanley Wells and Gary Taylor. 2nd ed. Oxford: Oxford University Press, 2005.

———. *Venus and Adonis*. In Wells and Taylor, *Oxford Shakespeare*.

Percy Bysshe Shelley. "Ode to the West Wind." In *The Poetry and Prose of Percy Bysshe Shelley*, edited by Neil Fraistat and Donald H. Reiman. 2nd ed. New York: W. W. Norton, 2002.

[George] Bernard Shaw. "Keats." In *The John Keats Memorial Volume*. London: John Lane, 1921.

Dorothy Van Ghent. *Keats: The Myth of the Hero*. Revised and edited by Jeffrey Cane Robinson. Princeton, NJ: Princeton University Press, 1983.

William Wordsworth. Preface to the 1800 edition of *Lyrical Ballads*. In *Wordsworth's Poetry and Prose*, edited by Nicholas Halmi. New York: W. W. Norton, 2014.

William Butler Yeats. "Ego Dominus Tuus." In *The Collected Poems of W. B. Yeats*, edited by Richard J. Finneran. New York: Macmillan, 1989.

Ode to a Nightingale

My heart aches, and a drowsy numbness pains
  My sense, as though of hemlock I had drunk,
Or emptied some dull opiate to the drains
  One minute past, and Lethe-wards[1] had sunk:
'Tis not through envy of thy happy lot,
  But being too happy in thine happiness,—
    That thou, light-winged Dryad[2] of the trees
      In some melodious plot
Of beechen green, and shadows numberless,
  Singest of summer in full-throated ease.

O, for a draught of vintage! that hath been
  Cool'd a long age in the deep-delved earth,
Tasting of Flora[3] and the country green,
  Dance, and Provençal song, and sunburnt mirth!
O for a beaker full of the warm South,

(1) In Greek mythology, Lethe is a river in the underworld that causes
all who drink from it to forget the world of the living.
(2) A forest nymph.
(3) The goddess of flowering plants.

Full of the true, the blushful Hippocrene[4],
   With beaded bubbles winking at the brim,
     And purple-stained mouth;
That I might drink, and leave the world unseen,
   And with thee fade away into the forest dim:

Fade far away, dissolve, and quite forget
   What thou among the leaves hast never known,
The weariness, the fever, and the fret
   Here, where men sit and hear each other groan;
Where palsy shakes a few, sad, last gray hairs,
   Where youth grows pale, and spectre-thin, and dies;
     Where but to think is to be full of sorrow
      And leaden-eyed despairs,
Where Beauty cannot keep her lustrous eyes,
   Or new Love pine at them beyond to-morrow.

Away! away! for I will fly to thee,
   Not charioted by Bacchus and his pards[5],
But on the viewless wings of Poesy,
   Though the dull brain perplexes and retards:
Already with thee! tender is the night,
   And haply the Queen-Moon is on her throne,
     Cluster'd around by all her starry Fays[6];
     But here there is no light,
Save what from heaven is with the breezes blown
   Through verdurous glooms and winding mossy ways.

(4) A fountain sacred to the Nine Muses and thus a source of poetic inspiration.
(5) That is, by the god of wine and revelry and the leopards said to draw his chariot.
(6) Fairies.

I cannot see what flowers are at my feet,
　　Nor what soft incense hangs upon the boughs,
But, in embalmed darkness, guess each sweet
　　Wherewith the seasonable month endows
The grass, the thicket, and the fruit-tree wild;
　　White hawthorn, and the pastoral eglantine;
　　　　Fast fading violets cover'd up in leaves;
　　　　　　And mid-May's eldest child,
The coming musk-rose, full of dewy wine,
　　　　The murmurous haunt of flies on summer eves.

Darkling[7] I listen; and, for many a time
　　I have been half in love with easeful Death,
Call'd him soft names in many a mused rhyme,
　　To take into the air my quiet breath;
Now more than ever seems it rich to die,
　　To cease upon the midnight with no pain,
　　　　While thou art pouring forth thy soul abroad
　　　　　　In such an ecstasy!
Still wouldst thou sing, and I have ears in vain—
　　To thy high requiem become a sod.

Thou wast not born for death, immortal Bird!
　　No hungry generations tread thee down;
The voice I hear this passing night was heard
　　In ancient days by emperor and clown:
Perhaps the self-same song that found a path
　　Through the sad heart of Ruth[8], when, sick for home,
　　　　She stood in tears amid the alien corn;

(7) An archaic adverb meaning "growing dark."
(8) A heroine of the Old Testament who remains with her in-laws after
her husband dies, far from her own homeland.

The same that oft-times hath
Charm'd magic casements[9], opening on the foam
Of perilous seas, in faery lands forlorn.

Forlorn! the very word is like a bell
To toll me back from thee to my sole self!
Adieu! the fancy cannot cheat so well
As she is fam'd to do, deceiving elf.
Adieu! adieu! thy plaintive anthem fades
Past the near meadows, over the still stream,
Up the hill-side; and now 'tis buried deep
In the next valley-glades:
Was it a vision, or a waking dream?
Fled is that music:—Do I wake or sleep?

In Room 18 of the National Portrait Gallery, London, Keats sits on one cane chair with his elbow propped on another, reading. The book on his lap looks to be in octavo format, standard size at the time for the everyman's library. Because his lap is small, his entire frame petite, the book takes up a surprising amount of room. Keats's legs are crossed, and his left hand rests near the crown of his head, and if his expression weren't so placid the attitude might betray something like despair. Minimally, it is the gesture of a person in the middle of a conversation he doesn't want to have. Perhaps he feels self-conscious being looked at for so long, but this is impossible: when Joseph Severn finished the portrait, Keats had been dead for two years.

Severn was with Keats for the last three months of his life. Despite not being a close friend of the poet's, and despite hav-

(9) Windows.

ing a reputation in their shared circle as something of a limp noodle, Severn alone agreed to accompany the ailing Keats to Rome, where—the idea was—he might convalesce in the warm southern air. After a difficult journey, including ten days quarantined on a ship in the Bay of Naples, where a typhus epidemic was raging, Keats and Severn took up residence at 26 Piazza di Spagna, in a tiny apartment next to the Spanish Steps. There was some effort to pretend this was just a vacation, though Keats's medical training told him he had hardly at any time left.

At some point they rented a piano, because Severn was an able pianist, and Keats loved music. An English doctor by the name of Clark put Keats on a starvation diet of milk, bread, and from time to time a single bite of fish; he wasn't convinced Keats had what we now call tuberculosis, because most of the consumptives he'd seen were enervated and withdrawn, whereas Keats was frenzied, almost hyperactive. The new diagnosis was a nervous complaint, the result of overzealous "mental exertions and applications"—in a word, stress. One morning in December Keats coughed up two cups of blood "black and thick in the extreme." Clark drained him of another eight ounces while Severn hid the knives and the laudanum, terrified that the patient—who had no scruples against suicide—would kill himself on his watch. Keats's mind, Severn wrote to a friend, formed "despair in every shape."

For the next several weeks, in a room the size of a large closet, Keats would wander in and out of a screaming delirium, "a wreck of his former self." He'd speculate that poetry had been the death of him, or else his failure to consummate the relationship with Brawne, whose letters he refused to open; they're buried in his grave in Rome's Protestant Cemetery, the only letters from her to him whose location is known. He drove Severn up the wall with his demand for new books, and despite his increasingly vocal contempt for Christianity ("I think a malignant being must have power over us, over whom the Almighty has little or no influence"), he was determined to get his hands on a copy of *The Rule and Exercises of Holy Dying*, a consolatory treatise published in 1651 by the Anglican cleric Jeremy Taylor. But the book was not to be had, and that's for the best, for Keats would surely have spit fire at Taylor's judgment that "nothing is intolerable that is necessary." Somehow he never lost his sense of humor: seeing that Severn was composing a letter to one of his publishers, John Taylor, Keats cackled, "Tell Taylor I shall soon be in a second edition—in sheets—and cold dress."

The Keats of Severn's portrait is remembered in pain, with a downturned mouth and a heaviness around the eyelids, as if he is trying not to cry. It's more of a death mask than Keats's actual death mask, a plaster cast you can see, today, at the museum that the apartment at 26 Piazza di Spagna has become. It's more unsettling, too, than the little ink sketch Severn did of Keats as he lay dying, because, in the National Gallery portrait, we get the sense that this was someone who had long been living what Keats himself called "a posthumous existence"— a pantomime of vitality stretched out long past some early dissolution. He must have always had that look: a face full of water. Even here, reading quietly on a sunny afternoon, in a neat black suit and shiny black shoes, reddish-brown hair beautifully combed, he looks seasick, perilously close to self-cancellation.

A lot about Keats was light, and light clung to him. His world was full of parties and jokes, and his reputation for kindness was such that, even when it was clear his case was terminal, his closest friends were still hitting him up for money. Nonetheless, in Severn's dream-autopsy of the person he was before he became terminally ill, drenched in sunshine with Shakespeare's portrait watching over him, Keats curves into a world from which his entire middle tenderly recoils. It's a body primed for experience to break it, and that will be easy, because it is already half broken, had been from a time literally immemorial. His presence flickers, hurt.

Even Keats's what-ifs trail into omission. In the last letter he would ever write, he starts to put down some thoughts about Brawne before staggering backward: "God knows how it would have been—but it appears to me—however, I will not speak of that subject." This reserve speaks less of an alternative too painful to contemplate than one unable to cohere; if despair came to Keats in every shape, happiness remained for him an obscure hypothetical, perhaps even less than that. Near death or never near enough to life, he couldn't shake his conviction that the intolerable would always be necessary, the only sure and certain thing.

*

"Ode to a Nightingale" glimpses a posthumous existence inside a regular one and lives to tell the tale. It is a worrisome, even frightening poem whose self-destructive impulses are to some extent camouflaged by its beauty. When we walk away from it, it's the beauty we remember, much more than the painful encounter with a person on the very edge of finding life supportable. This is deliberate. One of Keats's favorite themes is the persistence of beauty within the ugliest situations, from intimate anguish to political crisis. In this case, he wants us to think about how poetic language both makes vivid and distracts us from the commonplace reality of someone suffering, unspectacularly, right before our very eyes.

Charles Brown, Keats's friend and long-time roommate, tells a story about Keats composing the ode while listening to a nightingale that had built a nest just outside their house:

> In the spring of 1819 a nightingale had built her nest near [the] house. Keats felt a tranquil and continual joy in her song; and one morning he took his chair from the breakfast-table to the grass-plot under a plum-tree, where he sat for two or three hours. When he came into the house, I perceived he had some scraps of paper in his hand, and these he was quietly thrusting behind the books. On inquiry, I found those scraps, four or five in number, contained his poetic feeling on the song of the nightingale. The writing was not well legible; and it was difficult to arrange the stanzas on so many scraps. With his assistance I succeeded, and this was his "Ode to a Nightingale," a poem which has been the delight of everyone.

What's interesting about Brown's anecdote is that it so perfectly models a bad—or, at the very least, extremely naive—reading of Keats's poem, which is neither tranquil nor joyous and which, if it is indeed "a delight to everyone," is far from a delight to itself.

The baseline measure of Keats's odes is iambic pentameter, but the first line of this ode is already off the rails. We won't get too technical here, but notice how the first three words push back against the perky, rational rhythm of a standard iambic line, which follows an unstressed by a stressed syllable. Arguably all of the first three (and certainly the second and third) syllables are stressed, which lends them the air of being slow, plodding. Their lugubrious sound suits the sense: it is elongated, like the insistent discomfort described by the word "ache" and drowsy, like the numbness this first line paradoxically calls a pain. If Brown wants the ode to reflect Keats's mood upon its writing—exhilarated, jolly, quick—he has another thing coming.

This is a slow poem, in which every exquisite phrase falls like a hand of cards softly folded. It is also quiet or, in Keats's words, a "quiet breath." Throughout the ode Keats is extraordinarily careful with his caesuras: pauses within the line instead of at the end of it. There is one right after "aches" and, in the second line, right after "sense." The effect is to establish, right off the bat, a verse that moves in the undulating, slightly irregular rhythm of what Keats elsewhere calls the "tender-taken breath" of sleep.

That unevenness appears, too, in the structure of the stanzas, with their abbreviated eighth lines. It is a raspy, hobbled, tired poem with a strong desire to disappear—to "fade far away and dissolve" not even into words but into the space between them. What it wants, in other words, is a version of the longing the psychoanalyst Heinz Kohut attributes to a patient annoyed by the way his analyst breathes: "he is searching for some kind of environment that is so tuned into him that it doesn't make any noise at all[.]"

In this frame of mind, the pleasure of others is a singular affront. Consider this complaint: *too happy in thine happiness*. The preposition "in" is doing a lot of work. Not happy *because of* thine happiness (that would be the "envy" option, already dismissed), not happy *through* or *with* thine happiness (too companionate, too consensual), but too happy *in* thine happiness—caught in the spokes, sped up, made sick. It's a version of a thought Keats will express to Brawne as he draws closer to his departure for Italy: "I do not think my health will improve much while I am separated from you" and yet "for all this I am averse to seeing you—I cannot bear flashes of light and return into my glooms again."

The irritation sparked by the nightingale is muted but

much the same, and it's worth noting that both this poem and Keats's letter climax in nearly twin expressions of the suicidal urge: "Now more than ever seems it rich to die" and, to Brawne, "Hamlet's heart was full of such Misery as mine is when he said to Ophelia 'Go to a Nunnery, go, go!' Indeed I should like to give up the matter at once—I should like to die." There are two forms of extinction in play here: Brawne must be dead to pleasure so that Keats can be dead, period, her absence an alibi for his more general dissatisfaction.

In the ode, that same cruel logic is captured in a roll call of negations—*unseen, viewless, no light, not born*—that strike out all possibility of moving toward life instead of resigning from it. It's a rhetorical strategy that surfaces a hundred and twenty years later in Charles Olson's "In Cold Hell, in Thicket," another poem of "cold doing" that condenses deep psychic turmoil in privative grammatical forms:

> How shall he who is not happy, who has been so made
>   unclear,
> who is no longer privileged to be at ease, who, in this brush,
>   stands
> reluctant, imageless, unpleasured, caught in a sort of hell,
>   how
> shall he convert this underbrush, how turn this unbidden
>   place
> how trace and arch again
> the necessary goddess?

Olson's brush and underbrush are Keats's melodious "plot," a word that signifies both a piece of land and a grave. His goddess (as the rest of the poem makes clear) is "space," and Keats is out of that too, or at least it's beyond his sight. What remains is a scarcely muted hum of rage and its secret whim to strike everything, including one's own self, out. Its softness and slowness match what Olson calls the "dissolving bones" of that desire; whatever they touch fades to black.

*

Keats's ode is often paired with Samuel Taylor Coleridge's poem "The Nightingale," first published in the 1798 version of *Lyrical Ballads*, a collection of poems co-authored with Wordsworth. There are certainly a few similarities between the poems, the most obvious being that both poets have no interest in symbolism. This is surprising, since the nightingale is traditionally associated not only with poetry but also with extreme distress, of the sort described by Keats's third stanza.

In Ovid's *Metamorphoses*, a young woman named Philomela is raped by her brother-in-law, who cuts out her tongue to stop her from revealing his crime. In revenge, Philomela and her sister kill her nephew, cook him, and feed him to his father. Ultimately Philomela, her brother-in-law, and her sister are all changed by the gods into birds, Philomela into the nightingale that hides itself in the dark forest. The story all but identifies poetry with pain and specifically with sexual violence—a subject Keats will treat more fully in his "Ode on a Grecian Urn."

Taking a cue from Coleridge, who says the tale of Philomela is just too heavy to project onto a poor little bird, Keats doesn't go anywhere near the themes it raises. But he's also not interested in arguing, as Coleridge does, for a view of nature free from all the trappings of myth. On the contrary, "Ode to a Nightingale" is full of classical allusions, all of which suggest the poet's fatigue, even his disgust, at his own erudition. This poet knows things, for sure: the names of streams (Lethe, Hippocrene) you drink from to forget your life, of nymphs and gods and biblical heroines sick for home. He also knows some things about nature, like which flowers bloom at certain times of the day and how they smell, even in the city's stale breezes. This trivia orbits him; he plucks bits of it out of the air like dandelion fuzz. But beneath this haze of small intelligences, he is losing his will to think.

Keats's greater debt, by far, is to another poem by Coleridge called "Dejection: An Ode." Coleridge initially wrote "Dejection" about his ill-starred love for Sara Hutchinson—Wordsworth's sister-in-law—but the poem gathered steam until it became an indictment of Wordsworth's many betrayals of their friendship. Despite all this, it would be wrong to say that "Dejection" is spurred by any one particular heartbreak or misfortune. It is, rather, an extraordinary poem about how depression—the modern word for "dejection"—causes us, in Eve Kosofsky Sedgwick's words, to "stop knowing / how to like and desire / the world around us." Coleridge's dejection, in other words, is not really anyone's fault. It is a more or less perpetual state of extreme and extremely painful isolation punctuated by the appearance of other people, who might seem, at first, to make it better but will inevitably make it worse.

Dejection is stronger than *melancholy*, a manic and loquacious sorrow Keats will handle in another one of the Great Odes. It is virulently anti-social, something you can hear even in the name. If *depression* implies the general sensation of being crushed, *dejection* gives that sensation a cause: it's what happens when you're cast out and down, when you've been denied, or feel you've been denied, the love and understanding of others. Most alarmingly—and this is what Sedgwick gets at too—it produces apathy or anesthesia, reducing our innate sensitivity to beauty to a lank, bone-dry perception. "All this long eve, so balmy and serene," writes Coleridge, "Have I been gazing on the western sky . . . and with how blank an eye!"

And those thin clouds above, in flakes and bars,
That give away their motion to the stars;
Those stars, that glide behind them or between,
Now sparkling, now bedimmed, but always seen:
Yon crescent Moon, as fixed as if it grew
In its own cloudless, starless lake of blue;
I see them all so excellently fair,
I see, not feel, how beautiful they are!

Keats runs this logic exactly in reverse to reach the same con-
clusion. If Coleridge flinches at his own detachment, Keats—
ever the irrepressible sensualist—treats dejection as a narcotic
state of being that is paradoxically loud, lavish, and full. Even
its numbness stings.

It is not an insult to say that dejection is anti-social. In fact,
that is probably its best quality, if we understand *anti-social*
to mean committed to refusing things as they are; "I am sick-
ened," Keats told Brawne, "at the brute world which you are
smiling with." Neither Keats's poem nor Coleridge's builds into
an attack on what Theodor Adorno so memorably calls "wrong
life"—which, he says, "cannot be lived rightly"—but both do
draw a restless connection between individual suffering and
our pitiful human estate. The third stanza of Keats's ode like-
wise lurches out of private reverie to deliver a scathing com-
ment on an existence "where but to think is to be full of sor-
row," while Coleridge shudders as he imagines the "groans, of
trampled men, with smarting wounds" or else a little girl who
"now moans low in bitter grief and fear, / And now screams
loud, and hopes to make her mother hear."

Keats and Coleridge are both playing off of Milton's ac-
count, in *Paradise Lost*, of Adam glimpsing the future that orig-
inal sin has wrought. Instead of living in peace and abundance,
mankind—ejected, or *dejected*, from Eden—is thrown into a

life of physical and mental anguish, subject to "maladies / of ghastly spasm, or racking torture, qualms / of heartsick agony" and so on. The whole world looks, from this vantage, like a "Lazar-house": a quarantine hospital where Death, instead of being feared, is "oft invoked" as a "chief good, and final hope." We hear Milton in Keats's short rundown of "the weariness, the fever, and the fret" that strikes old men with palsy and wastes the young, and we hear him too, in this picture of death as a deliverer, cajoled in "soft names" to visit Keats more quickly. "Now more than ever seems it rich to die" is the exhausted end-point of Adam's "Better end here unborn." Neither gets his way.

Keats was surely reminded of Milton's Lazar-house during his days as a medical student, when he assisted at amputations, primitive surgeries, and the care of all those beyond hope. He was likely reminded of it, too, at the deathbed of his younger brother Tom, who died, as Keats would, from tuberculosis, the highly contagious bacterial disease that primarily attacks the lungs, shredding their fragile tissues. In the nineteenth century, TB was still called "consumption" because of the way it seemed to eat people alive, causing not only a characteristic hacking cough but also sudden and extreme weight loss. Medical treatises from Keats's era frequently quote a description of consumptive patients given by Aretaeus of Cappadocia, a Greek physician of the first century C.E.: "The whole body is shrivelled: the spine projects, instead of sinking, from the decay of the muscles; and the shoulder blades stand out like the wings of birds."

The last days of Tom, Keats reported, "were of the most distressing nature; but his last moments were not so painful, and he died without a pang." Within six months, Keats will have written a poem—about birds, and their wings—that not only longs to "cease upon the midnight with no pain" but that positively revels in the work of deleting sensation altogether.

To be clear, nothing about the poem betrays a hope to inter-
vene in the racking tortures of wrong life. Its first priority is
to relieve Keats and nobody else. There's a reason why Phi-
lomela doesn't feature more prominently here; there's a rea-
son, too, why the hungry generations who cramp and cry out
"here, where men sit and hear each other groan" are so vaguely
drawn. Keats, for nearly the entire duration of this poem, is
already half-gone from them and from what they represent.
He has, in other words, one foot in that ice-bound place where
other people exist only as confirmations that Keats would be
better off dead. As Olson says,

> (this is why he of whom we speak does not move, why
> he stands so awkward where he is, why
> his feet are held, like some ragged crane's
> off the nearest next ground[.]

*

For the reader who has been following the ode closely, who has
heard in its references to poisons and opiates and its insistently
negative vocabulary (*unseen, not born*, etc.) a five-alarm fire of
suicidal ideation, the sixth stanza has the force less of a con-
fession than a dare, not far off from a *fuck you*. The poem has
backed us into a corner, as disclosures of this kind often do. It
has stolen our pleasure in it, because what would it mean to call
a poem like this beautiful, to act like its elegance and virtuosity
could be enjoyed apart from the death wish it records? It would
mean, Keats says, becoming a sod: a clump of earth and also
an idiot, as insensible to grief as dejection is insensible to joy.

The reprieve of the last stanza is small but significant, and
it involves the reader directly. Up until this point, the object
of Keats's address has been the nightingale: "Thou wast not

born for death, immortal Bird," "I will fly to thee," and so on. In the last stanza, however, his apostrophe is split between the nightingale and us. Keats waves goodbye to the bird three times ("Adieu! ... Adieu! adieu!") and then pronounces its music "fled." With a colon and a dash the poem's last five words are sawed off from everything that precedes them, the punctuation operating here like a stage direction or cue, as Keats turns to direct his final question to us: "Do I wake or sleep?"

The question is insignificant, but asking it isn't. At the very last minute, Keats finds his footing in the world once more. He looks for someone, talks to them, abandoning, at least for now, the misanthropic posture of the foregoing stanzas for a more sociable conclusion. There is plenty of irony in the fact that the word that prompts this change of heart is "forlorn," not just sad but abandoned and alone. Although Keats says that its sound returns him to his sole self, it seems, on the contrary, to return him to the presence of some other standing by.

The doubling of the word across two stanzas ("forlorn" closes out the seventh stanza and opens up the eighth) has a similar effect: *forlorn*, said twice, is forlorn no more, and when Keats repeats the word for us he is repeating it in a changed mood. These last ten lines are conspicuously crisper ("like a bell") and more orderly than the seventy that precede them, as if the poem has abruptly decided to pull itself together. It tilts, at its end, from outsize feeling to more manageable action: sleeping and waking, the unremarkable rhythms of remarkable survival.

When Kohut tells that story about the patient who can't stand his analyst's breathing, he's doing something any good reader does: he is paying attention. In practice this means hearing the hope behind the complaint, the need behind the demand, just as the good reader gives the text back to itself in a slightly altered expanded form. The patient wants a silence that matches his own desolation, and Keats wants an audience among which, even terminally "sole," he can still keep the final option at bay. Good reading does not try to argue with desire—to tell Keats, for example, that it is never rich to die, since sometimes it surely is. After all, Kohut observes, when we're dealing with someone who has "expressed something sensitively, maybe foolishly...to embarrass him by telling him that it is nonsense is just as nonsensical as trying to say 'Yes I will try not to breathe.'"

It is unreasonable to be asked not to breathe. But it is miraculous to breathe for another.

Sources

Theodor Adorno. *Minima Moralia: Reflections on Damaged Life*. London: Verso, 2006.

Charles Armitage Brown. *Life of Keats*. Edited by Dorothy Hyde Bodurtha and W. B. Pope. London: Oxford University Press, 1937.

Sue Brown. *Joseph Severn, a Life: The Rewards of Friendship*. Oxford: Oxford University Press, 2009.

John Keats. "Bright star, would I were as steadfast as thou art." In *Complete Poems*, edited by Jack Stillinger. Cambridge, MA: Harvard University Press, 1982.

———. Letter to Fanny Brawne, dated 8 August 1820. In *The Letters of John Keats*, vol. 2, edited by Hyder Edward Rollins. 2 vols. Cambridge, MA: Harvard University Press, 1958.

———. Letter to Charles Brown, dated 30 November 1820. In Rollins, *Letters of John Keats*, vol. 2.

———. Letter to George and Georgiana Keats, dated 18 December 1818. In Rollins, *Letters of John Keats*, vol. 1.

Heinz Kohut. "Lecture 7, March 29, 1974: On the Therapeutic Alliance." In *The Chicago Institute Lectures*, ed. Paul Tolpin and Marian Tolpin. Hillsdale, NJ: Analytic Press, 1996.

John Milton. *Paradise Lost*. In *Complete Poems and Major Prose*, ed. Merritt Y. Hughes. New York: Macmillan, 1957.

Charles Olson. "In Cold Hell, in Thicket." In *Selected Poems of Charles Olson*, ed. Robert Creeley. Berkeley: University of California Press, 1997.

Eve Kosofsky Sedgwick. *Fat Art/Thin Art*. Durham, NC: Duke University Press, 1994.

Jeremy Taylor. *The Rule and Exercises of Holy Dying*. 2nd ed. London: R. Royston, 1652.

Thomas Young. *A Practical and Historical Treatise on Consumptive Diseases, Deduced from Original Observations, and Collected from Authors of All Ages*. London: Underwood, 1815.

Ode on a Grecian Urn

Thou still unravish'd bride of quietness,
    Thou foster-child of silence and slow time,
Sylvan[1] historian, who canst thus express
    A flowery tale more sweetly than our rhyme:
What leaf-fring'd legend haunts about thy shape
    Of deities or mortals, or of both,
        In Tempe or the dales of Arcady[2]?
    What men or gods are these? What maidens loth?
What mad pursuit? What struggle to escape?
        What pipes and timbrels[3]? What wild ecstasy?

Heard melodies are sweet, but those unheard
    Are sweeter; therefore, ye soft pipes, play on;
Not to the sensual ear, but, more endear'd,
    Pipe to the spirit ditties of no tone:
Fair youth, beneath the trees, thou canst not leave
    Thy song, nor ever can those trees be bare;
        Bold Lover, never, never canst thou kiss,

(1) Rural or pastoral.
(2) The Vale of Tempe and Arcady (or Arcadia) are regions of Greece
associated with unspoiled wilderness.
(3) Tambourines.

Though winning near the goal—yet, do not grieve;
  She cannot fade, though thou hast not thy bliss,
 For ever wilt thou love, and she be fair!

Ah, happy, happy boughs! that cannot shed
 Your leaves, nor ever bid the spring adieu;
And, happy melodist, unwearied,
 For ever piping songs for ever new;
More happy love! more happy, happy love!
 For ever warm and still to be enjoy'd,
  For ever panting, and for ever young;
All breathing human passion far above,
 That leaves a heart high-sorrowful and cloy'd,
  A burning forehead, and a parching tongue.

Who are these coming to the sacrifice?
 To what green altar, O mysterious priest,
Lead'st thou that heifer lowing at the skies,
 And all her silken flanks with garlands drest?
What little town by river or sea shore,
 Or mountain-built with peaceful citadel,
  Is emptied of this folk, this pious morn?
And, little town, thy streets for evermore
 Will silent be; and not a soul to tell
  Why thou art desolate, can e'er return.

O Attic[4] shape! Fair attitude! with brede
 Of marble men and maidens overwrought,
With forest branches and the trodden weed;
 Thou, silent form, dost tease us out of thought
As doth eternity: Cold Pastoral!

(4) Attic means Athenian; the sense here is of something belonging to the Greek Classical Period.

When old age shall this generation waste,
    Thou shalt remain, in midst of other woe
  Than ours, a friend to man, to whom thou say'st,
    "Beauty is truth, truth beauty," — that is all
    Ye know on earth, and all ye need to know.

Even the first word sounds like an assault. Keats dispenses with the usual invocatory "O" and with it a baseline of respect—the adulation proper to the ode. This is more of a hey-you or a catcall and, like a catcall, it has an air of substantial menace. It also carries a cry of pain, the *ow* in *Thou*, a name spun around a moan. Instantly the poem's object is designated by hurt indivisible from the condition of being an other, a *you* and not an *I*. Keats begins no other poem this way, and while all his odes— while all odes—have the structure of unanswered address, this one specially figures address as an act of aggression. If this poem were a street you would hope to avoid walking down it.

Another thing that distinguishes this poem is that its speaker is not Keats but a character or persona. This is a controversial position but I'm taking it anyway. You might agree with me once it becomes clear that what this speaker is saying is singularly abhorrent, though it does take some work to get there. The poem has factored in plenty of clues, and *Thou* is its first. It is a sour note and an alarm call, but only to those who know how to hear it. As for the ode itself, it is an extremely subversive meditation on just who knows how to hear what, and on who is responsible for what Amiri Baraka (writing as LeRoi Jones) calls "the silence of starving talk."

The silence of starving talk or, as Keats puts it, the unheard melody. Reading "Ode to a Nightingale," we expected a visit from Philomela, the woman whose rapist cuts out her tongue to prevent her from telling her story and whom the gods—as both salvation and punishment—turn into a bird. We didn't get it, and if that myth hangs in the background of that poem, it is only one part of an unimaginably vast history of human suffering, from ancient times down to the present impossible day. "Ode on a Grecian Urn," however, wants to talk about that history in a way that is more precise, even specialized. It is, to put it bluntly, a poem about sexual violence. More broadly—and more uncomfortably—it is a poem about poetry's long involvement in a cultural tradition that takes sexual violence to be an especially rich source of inspiration for art.

In an essay collected in his book, *The Long Schoolroom: Lessons in the Bitter Logic of the Poetic Principle*, Allen Grossman suggests that the story of Philomela is, along with the story of Orpheus, one of two foundational myths describing the personal and moral difficulty of poetry. It's a gendered difficulty, says Grossman, that establishes a sturdy if also limited and tiresome division between masculine and feminine types of "song." Masculine poetry, or the song of Orpheus, is about the experience of being orphaned by love and turning, by way of compensation, to nature, which is not at all natural but rather a world the poet coerces into being. Feminine poetry, or the song of Philomela, is about pain. It is "omnipresent in history in the same way that pain is omnipresent in history," and therefore anterior to Orpheus's narrative, "always already there, even as witness."

The obligation to represent pain thus falls disproportionately on art about female anguish, especially when it is caused, as Philomela's is, by sexual abuse. You'll notice that Keats's speaker begins by calling the urn a bride, instantly feminizing it. But before he does that, he does something even more unsettling: he calls the urn "still unravished," one of the most ominous adjectival phrases in English literary history, right up there with the title and first line of Robert Browning's "My Last Duchess." In Browning's poem, *last* means "most recent." It tips us off that the speaker is a serial killer, with a long line of duchesses who've met the same gruesome fate and one or more duchesses on deck who'll go that way too. "Still unravished" similarly implies that harm to the bride is imminent.

If the poem begins with a yowl of pain, "unravished" specifies the cause of the injury. The word comes from the Latin verb *rapere*, to seize. Its use to describe assault goes back to the Middle Ages, when the rape of women was categorized as a property crime (the theft of someone's daughter, wife, sister, mother, etc.). Interestingly, the Romantic period is so called because it overlapped with a surge of interest in medieval romances—long poems or novels written, according to an influential essay by the eighteenth-century scholar Richard Hurd, to process social anxieties about rape. The Middle Ages, Hurd says, were a brutal time, during which the threat of sexual violence would have been perpetual. By celebrating the chivalric commitment to defending women at all costs, the romance created a fantasy world to make up—however feebly—for the horrors of the real one.

Whatever we make of this thesis, it lends a certain irony to the fact that "Ode on a Grecian Urn" is so often considered the quintessential Romantic poem. The scene on the urn doesn't show a rape, but neither does it show a rape miraculously averted. The poem is an *ekphrasis* or description of a work of art—in this case, of a work of art within a work of art, for Keats gives us not the shape or height or build of the urn but rather its design. That design consists of a picture of a religious gathering, with a formal procession of priests and sacrificial animals. Somewhere, off to the side perhaps, women are being chased by men. These women, or maidens, are "loth," which means unwilling or, more strongly, hating what you are being forced to do; that is why they "struggle to escape" and also why the heifer, or a young female cow, is found several lines later "lowing," in a protest against her fate that is also a half-rhyme for the menacing sound of *thou*.

These are all Keats's words, and yet very few scholars have called this image what it is. What it is—what Keats knows it is—is an image of a rape about to take place. This is true of those maidens loth, and it is true of the encounter spotlighted in the second stanza, in which the poem speaks of a "bold lover" chasing down someone referred to only as "the goal." Helen Vendler sees this image and that of the maidens loth as offering two contrasting visions of sexuality: one violent, the other "entirely idyllic." *Entirely* is an overstatement. Even if you decided not to see the chase as continuous with the "mad pursuit" of the first stanza it would still be happening in a world where the first stanza happens.

(If you wanted to opt for an even more benign reading of the "bold lover" passage and take the chase as a bit of light-hearted consensual lovers' play, you would still have to ask: Is being left "forever panting," forever held at bay from bliss, actually ideal? Or merely picturesque?)

The urn is not Achilles's shield, that magical artifact which (according to Homer) collapses time and space to show the city of peace and the city of war, order and chaos, joy and despair all at the same time. The urn's picture is cramped and concurrent; everyone here comes from one little town. This is one place, one moment, stuck fast forever. If the urn is a freeze-frame of things that never come to pass, it also a memorial to what never seems to end.

*

The bold lover who can never, never kiss and the person who runs from him are lifted right out of Ovid's *Metamorphoses*, which was completed around 8 CE. The *Metamorphoses* is an epic poem organized around a single subject—change—and it takes shape over a long series of two hundred and fifty or so stories in which a being is transformed into another kind of being. It is striking, and utterly unavoidable, how many of these stories turn on chase scenes exactly like the one Keats describes, in which a maiden loth is pursued by a determined man. It is also striking how repetitious Ovid's language can be. Philomela is pursued by her brother-in-law Tereus the way a rabbit is hunted by an eagle. The water nymph Arethusa, fleeing from the river god Alphaeus, is compared to a dove tailed by a hawk. Apollo breathes down Daphne's neck like a greyhound nipping at the heels of a hare:

> Now bears he [u]p; now, now he hopes to fetch her;
> And, with his snowt extended, straines to catch her:
> Not knowing whether caught or no, shee slips
> Out of his wide-stretcht [j]awes, and touching lips.
> The God and Virgin in such strife appeare:
> He, quickned by his hope; She, by her feare[.]

All of these chases end, eventually, with the maiden and sometimes the man undergoing a change of form. Philomela's change comes too late; it is only after her rape (and her murder of Tereus's son) that she becomes a nightingale. Arethusa escapes Alphaeus by becoming a lake, but he becomes one too, so he can lie next to her forever; her escape, in other words, is incomplete. Similarly, the nymph Syrinx becomes a bunch of reeds, which her would-be assailant, the god Pan, plucks and turns into a pair of pipes; "O sweet," Pan crows in George Sandys's 1632 translation, "together e[v]er thus con[v]erse will we." Daphne turns into a laurel tree, and Apollo, reaching his hand inside her trunk to wrap it around her still-pulsing heart, claims the laurel as his personal emblem; when he kisses her branches they pull away in disgust.

Ovid's *Metamorphoses*, then, is a poem about rape. It's about other things too, that are not unrelated: power and its abuses, desire and its asymmetries, art and its capacity (or lack thereof) to acknowledge that, as Fredric Jameson says, "the underside of culture is blood, torture, death and terror." That much should be clear to anyone who has read the poem, let alone read it seriously. "But," as Grossman reminds us, "there is good reading and there is bad reading." He goes further: "Bad reading is exemplified by the rapists' reading. The rapists read to find the 'pattern' of the crime they intend so they can repeat it. They read not to do otherwise but to do the same, and to learn how to escape doing's consequences."

This kind of reading, Grossman argues, takes representations of violence in works of art and repeats them—however indirectly—in real life. It is exactly the kind of reading or, to be precise, teaching described in a 2015 op-ed jointly authored by Kai Johnson, Tanika Lynch, Elizabeth Monroe, and Tracey Wang. The piece concerns a college course on Great Books, and recounts the experience of one student in it:

> During the week spent on Ovid's *Metamorphoses*, the class was instructed to read the myths of Persephone and Daphne, both of which include vivid depictions of rape and sexual assault. As a survivor of sexual assault, the student described being triggered while reading such detailed accounts of rape throughout the work. However, the student said her professor focused on the beauty of the language and the splendor of the imagery when lecturing on the text. As a result, the student

completely disengaged from the class discussion as a means of self-preservation. She did not feel safe in the class. When she approached her professor after class, the student said she was essentially dismissed, and her concerns were ignored.

As someone who has taught a course of exactly this kind and, for that matter, as a lover of Ovid, I find this account appalling. The *Metamorphoses* is a very beautiful poem, with many splendid images. Its significance as a work of art is partly due to these factors, but it is due in even greater measure to Ovid's head-on confrontation with the question of how aesthetic beauty coexists with or even depends upon violence, of which sexual violence is his exemplary case. If you miss that you've missed the poem completely, and the costs of this pedagogical failure redound, as they must, on the student. Her silence during discussion might be explained by Sandys, who says of Philomela, "Her mouth had lost the index of her wrong."

There has been much hand-wringing about so-called trigger or content warnings, which are meant to flag in advance if the material someone is about to encounter (especially in a classroom) might be especially upsetting or offensive. Those against trigger warnings often paint the students who want them as prudish and anti-intellectual, with no appreciation for the power and majesty of art. It seems to me that, on the contrary, the desire for trigger warnings expresses a fundamental belief that, in Grossman's words, "the practice of art is urgent and dangerous," because "what is at stake in the competition [to describe] human being is the value and status of the person in the cosmos and social order." To ask a teacher to hear a concern is to insist on the right to describe oneself, not to the exclusion of other descriptions but as a challenge to them. To

refuse to entertain those concerns is to undermine the status—
not just social but *cosmic*—of the person who does the asking.

*

The speaker of Keats's ode reads like a rapist. What else is that
ghastly assertion, "Beauty is truth, truth beauty" for but to de-
stroy the difference between a hypothetical harm and a real
one—to demand, in other words, that the aesthetic appeal of
the urn cleanse and redeem the horror it depicts? There's a lot
of editorial controversy over whether or not those are the only
lines in the poem the speaker attributes to the urn, or whether
the last thirteen words ("that is all/Ye know on earth, and all
ye need to know") are part of that projection. Hard to say: no
manuscript in Keats's handwriting survives, and there are lots
of other versions of the text floating about. For my part, I trust
the versions that follow the edition of Keats's poems printed
in 1820.

I trust it because it is in keeping with the rest of the poem,
in which the speaker identifies himself as precisely the kind of
person who would put that kind of statement, with its two-cent
profundity, into the mouth of the urn, as well as the kind of
person who would reserve for himself the flourish of the final
line and a half. He is dramatic, a loud talker who makes this
poem more of a monologue than an ode, more performance
than process. The sweep of the first four stanzas gives us the
sense of someone walking about the object he's describing, and
as each of the urn's pictures comes into view, he stops to item-
ize them: "What men or gods are these? What maidens loth?
What mad pursuit? What struggle to escape? What pipes and
timbrels? What wild ecstasy?"

What kind of questions are these? Rhetorical ones, de-
signed to be heard but not answered. It does not occur to the

speaker that they refer to disturbing events; it does not occur to him that his own language ("loth," "mad," "struggle," "escape," "wild") undercuts any suggestion that the events are less than catastrophic. To produce merely rhetorical questions in such a scenario is to wrest language from morality or, worse, to *try* and wrest language from morality, for the sake of an audience. That is what this speaker seems to think he has—an audience. His diction is elevated and pedantic, as if he's speaking to people either much older or slightly younger than himself; it has dressed to impress and it is conspicuously overdone, even by Keats's luxuriant standards. That's why it so often falters, as Keats finds little ways to sabotage him and to comment, even within the poem, on his absurd and malevolent reasoning.

Thus the syrupy phrases "Ah, happy, happy boughs" and "More happy love! more happy, happy love!" are pinned close to lines that describe their effects: it is these unfortunate exclamations that leave us "cloy'd" (stuffed, nauseated) or even poisoned ("burning forehead," "parching tongue"). The speaker's language has gotten ahead of him, saying much more than he means to say and knowing much more than he knows. This is the case with "unravished" and it is also true of "grieve" and "desolate," decidedly *un*happy words that point to the flipside of that Ovidian chase. The tragedy here is not that the girl never gets caught. It is the impossibly large tragedy of civilization itself, the long implacable history the speaker does not know he ought to lament.

Don't forget the repetition of "Attic/attitude," another oratorical embellishment reminding us this speaker loves, if nothing else, the sound of his own voice. This is in contrast to both the poem and the urn. The former is much happier to operate in the cloudy layer of ironies and double meanings, to stake its own moral claim precisely where the speaker abandons his. It lives in unheard melodies—in the true and unconscionable meaning of *loth* and *struggle* and *grieve* and *desolate*, subtly weakening the speaker's pretense that art means nothing but its own artistry, is utterly detached from the world whence its dark materials are drawn. As for the urn, it has said its piece, and prefers to sit in judgment. "You must be doing a lot of heavy thinking," Baraka observes, "to be so quiet."

*

In *Campus Sex, Campus Security*, her indispensable study of sexual violence and the rise of security culture in higher education, Jennifer Doyle argues that the mere idea of sex or sexuality being present on a college campus makes the institution lose its mind. Universities handle harassment and assault poorly, Doyle suggests, because they have worked so hard to pretend classrooms and dorms are not places where people have or act upon desire. The revelation that students have bodies as well as brains, that they can want sex and also be harmed by it or, most alarmingly, that they can perpetrate sexual harm, induces a kind of psychosis: a denial of definite reality.

That has certainly been my experience. I'll tell you about it, but first I want to talk more about Ovid, the first poet I ever read in a language not my own. My all-girls school had a robust Latin program, which almost all the students were hustled into around age thirteen. Keats, who could not read Greek, says that reading Homer in translation made him feel "like some watcher of the skies / When a new planet swims into his ken," and I felt the same translating Ovid, slowly but surely chipping away at the grammatical obscurities of case and number to find beneath verse so brash that any English version would thereafter feel sanitized or suppressed. I was infatuated, in particular, with Ovid's use of the word *remollescit*, which he leverages to describe a statue's marble thawing as the statue comes to life.

There's no good translation for it. It doesn't mean softens but *re*softens, softens then hardens, then softens again, reciprocal like living flesh.

By high school I had outpaced the official curriculum and was working alone to study for the two national Latin advance-placement exams. For the record, these were AP Latin: Virgil and AP Latin Literature: Catullus-Ovid; both exams have since been discontinued, due to a shortage of nerds. My senior year, the school hired a new Latin teacher, a self-satisfied bozo with thick fingers and a comically deep voice. In the first weeks of the fall semester, he kept me after class and told me he didn't get along with his wife. He preferred, he said, to have relationships with his attractive female students; that was the kind of relationship he would like to have with me. I laughed and scampered off to have a cigarette with my friends. It did not occur to me there was anything else to do.

Nor did it occur to my friends. To us, this proposal fell somewhere between black hole and old joke—it was mysterious but familiar, yet another sign that adult men were reliably foolish and disgusting, and that if we had to put up with their endless demands on our time we could at least get a good laugh out of it. The Latin teacher, despite receiving no signs of interest or encouragement, kept it up; of course he did. I started wearing thick, high-necked, oversized sweaters to class and taking the desk closest to the exit. It was an elaborate operation. A friend would linger in the room until the bell rang and ninety minutes later another would meet me at the door. The teacher snuck mash notes into vocabulary quizzes, compared me to Ovid's Daphne and Shakespeare's Rosalind. When it became clear he wouldn't be getting his way, he turned vengeful, marking my tests and essays down lower and lower each week until my hotshot conjugations were getting inexplicable Fs.

After he burst out screaming at me in class, I decided that

the pleasures of contempt were not worth this level of aggra-
vation. Passed swiftly up the food chain of school adminis-
trators, I soon landed in the office of our notoriously batty
headmistress, an ex-zoologist with one of those miscellaneous
Commonwealth accents: a little Australian, a little Canadian, a
lot British. The Latin teacher had explained to her that it was
all a misunderstanding. The trouble was that "the material"—
Virgil's *Aeneid*—lent itself "to a certain fudging of the bound-
aries." I was about to make a case for the *Aeneid* being one of
the least erotic poems imaginable, but she was ready with a
pitch. Unless I signed a statement absolving the school of any
responsibility, she would call the university that had admitted
me for next year and tell them to give my place to someone else.

I didn't sign, and she didn't, as far as I know, follow through.
Instead I was kicked out of Latin class and the teacher finished
out his year's contract before moving on to another school.
Two things came out of this experience. I never studied Latin
again, couldn't even look at it for a while without feeling phys-
ically ill. That was a great loss. I also learned how it feels to be
inconvenient, and that was a great gift. If I'd had another kind
of life, I would have been trained much earlier in the hard art
of becoming an obstacle. Instead I had enjoyed the lazy privi-
lege of thinking that being a good student would force the in-
stitution to leave me alone even when I acted up—that I would
be able, in a sense, to punch my own clock. I had thought, stu-
pidly, that I had outsmarted power, when in fact I hadn't yet
become a problem for it.

The *Metamorphoses* begins, "In nova fert animus muta-
tas dicere formas / corpora . . . ab origine mundi / ad mea . . .
tempora"—"my mind is made up to talk about bodies changed
into different forms, from the beginning of the world down to
my own time." A poem about bodies changed is also a poem
about what having a body changes. You stop speaking in class.

You sit in the back of rooms. You don't take walks at night. You lose a small but darling planet. If the epic of those metamorphoses were written, it would run in reverse, all the way back to the birth of the world, to the implosion of the first star.

*

In what is surely one of the strangest moments in the history of literary criticism, Kenneth Burke argues that we should replace the words "Beauty is truth, truth beauty" with "Body is turd, turd body." That, says Burke, is the real meaning of the poem, which is essentially a meditation on the fragility of our physical form and how pathetic it seems when compared to the longer-lasting, if not indestructible, forms of art. As far as I understand it (Burke is an extremely difficult writer), this doesn't seem too convincing. And yet Burke's got this much right: the urn is full of shit.

Well, not the urn, but the speaker who puts that piece of excremental wisdom in its mouth. His parting shot ("That is all ye know on earth . . .") shares an almost perfect reflective symmetry with the last line of the second stanza: "For ever wilt thou love, and she be fair." It's a kinship that knits the faux-philosophical slogan to the spectacle of what Anne Boyer calls "the suffering called gender named by capital as love." To agree with the urn's proclamation—again, it's really the speaker's—is to affirm a world in which harm and the threat of harm remain infinite even as they are covered up and brushed aside. It is to affirm a vision of masculinity as license to hurt and of femininity as perpetual provocation. All of this is unacceptable. If the poem were to accept it, it would not be a great poem. It would be a toast to the worst things anyone could say about poetry.

Keats has other plans for his ode. It is a critique, not a catechism: it does not want you to buy what its speaker is selling.

It gives him a platform and waits, like the urn, to see how we will respond. Will we choose to believe in an art that launders pain and calls that an ethics? Or will we opt for something else, not knowing necessarily what it might be but certain it will involve the loss of something precious—an elegant idea, a charming conceit, a way of being effortlessly in the world? If we choose that something else, it will be to embody the truth of an exchange Benjamin Robert Haydon recorded in his diary after he and Keats had been to see another classical relic, the Elgin Marbles: "We overheard two common looking decent men say to each other, 'How broken they are, a'ant they?' 'Yes,' said the other, 'but how *like life.*'"

Sources

Amiri Baraka (LeRoi Jones). "The Politics of Rich Painters." In *S.O.S: Poems, 1961–2013*. New York: Grove Press, 2014.

———. "Suppose Sorrow Was a Time Machine." In *Tales: Short Stories by Amiri Baraka*. Brooklyn: Akashic Books, 2016.

Anne Boyer. *A Handbook of Disappointed Fate*. Brooklyn: Ugly Duckling Presse, 2018.

Kenneth Burke. *A Rhetoric of Motives*. Berkeley: University of California Press, 1969.

Jennifer Doyle. *Campus Sex, Campus Security*. Cambridge, MA: MIT Press, 2015.

Allen Grossman. *The Long Schoolroom: Lessons in the Bitter Logic of the Poetic Principle*. Ann Arbor: University of Michigan Press, 1997.

Benjamin Robert Haydon. *Neglected Genius: The Diaries of Benjamin Robert Haydon*. Edited by John Jolliffe. London: Hutchinson, 1990.

Fredric Jameson. *Postmodernism; or, the Cultural Logic of Late Capitalism*. Durham, NC: Duke University Press, 1991.

Kai Johnson, Tanika Lynch, Elizabeth Monroe, and Tracey Wang. "Our identities matter in Core classrooms." *Columbia Daily Spectator*, 30 April 2015.

John Keats. "On First Looking into Chapman's Homer." In *Complete Poems*, edited by Jack Stillinger. Cambridge, MA: Harvard University Press, 1982.

Ovid (Publius Ovidius Naso). *Metamorphoses*. Edited by R. J. Tarrant. Oxford University Press, 2004.

George Sandys. *Ovid's Metamorphosis Englished: Oxford 1632*. New York: Garland, 1976.

Helen Vendler. *The Odes of John Keats*. Cambridge, MA: Harvard University Press, 1985.

Ode on Indolence

"They toil not, neither do they spin."

One morn before me were three figures seen,
  With bowed necks, and joined hands, side-faced;
And one behind the other stepp'd serene,
  In placid sandals, and in white robes graced:
They pass'd, like figures on a marble urn,
  When shifted round to see the other side;
    They came again; as when the urn once more
Is shifted round, the first seen shades return;
  And they were strange to me, as may betide
    With vases, to one deep in Phidian[1] lore.

How is it, shadows, that I knew ye not?
  How came ye muffled in so hush a masque?
Was it a silent deep-disguised plot
  To steal away, and leave without a task
My idle days? Ripe was the drowsy hour;
  The blissful cloud of summer-indolence

---

(1) Phidias is the sculptor believed (by some) to have created the Parthenon Marbles, also known as the Elgin Marbles.

Benumb'd my eyes; my pulse grew less and less;
Pain had no sting, and pleasure's wreath no flower.
O, why did ye not melt, and leave my sense
Unhaunted quite of all but—nothingness?

A third time pass'd they by, and, passing, turn'd
Each one the face a moment whiles to me;
Then faded, and to follow them I burn'd
And ached for wings, because I knew the three:
The first was a fair maid, and Love her name;
The second was Ambition, pale of cheek,
And ever watchful with fatigued eye;
The last, whom I love more, the more of blame
Is heap'd upon her, maiden most unmeek,—
I knew to be my demon[2] Poesy.

They faded, and, forsooth! I wanted wings:
O folly! What is Love? and where is it?
And for that poor Ambition—it springs
From a man's little heart's short fever-fit;
For Poesy!—no,—she has not a joy,—
At least for me,—so sweet as drowsy noons,
And evenings steep'd in honey'd indolence;
O, for an age so shelter'd from annoy,
That I may never know how change the moons,
Or hear the voice of busy common-sense!

A third time came they by;—alas! wherefore?
My sleep had been embroider'd with dim dreams;
My soul had been a lawn besprinkled o'er
With flowers, and stirring shades, and baffled beams:

(2) A spirit or supernatural being, neither malevolent nor benign.

The morn was clouded, but no shower fell,
    Though in her lids hung the sweet tears of May;
        The open casement[3] press'd a new-leaved vine,
    Let in the budding warmth and throstle's[4] lay;
O shadows! 'twas a time to bid farewell!
        Upon your skirts had fallen no tears of mine.

So, ye three ghosts, adieu! Ye cannot raise
    My head cool-bedded in the flowery grass;
For I would not be dieted with praise,
    A pet-lamb in a sentimental farce!
Fade softly from my eyes, and be once more
    In masque-like figures on the dreamy urn:
        Farewell! I yet have visions for the night,
And for the day faint visions there is store;
        Vanish, ye Phantoms! from my idle spright,
    Into the clouds, and never more return!

———————————

Barbara Browning's pensive sex comedy *The Correspondence Artist* begins with Vivian, a single mother, describing her romance with someone she refers to as "the paramour." Over the course of the novel, the paramour will assume the guises of four semi-plausible personae, from a young Vietnamese video artist to a sixty-eight-year-old lesbian writer with a girl in every port. The lovers—male and female, all ages and nationalities— are refractions, bouncing off an enigmatic source. All we really know about the paramour we glean from the features the four lovers share. Three of them are successful artists; all of them

(3) Window.
(4) A throstle is a thrush.

are famous. Their celebrity, Vivian explains, has its pros and cons:

> Since we live on different continents, our love affair has mostly been constituted by email exchanges. At times, our obsession with this process has seemed entirely mutual. At other times the paramour seems to get distracted. My dedication has been unflagging. It's partly fueled, I'm embarrassed to say, by the vain and yet stubborn belief that my overly informative and yet occasionally insightful missives might be feeding the creative process of a genius. I'm probably entirely mistaken. [My son] knows, of course, and he observes the relationship with wry detachment. This attitude helps me to remain detached as well.

This is the quintessence of Browning's narrative voice, itself a paradigm of wry detachment marbled through with a readiness for real love. Readiness but not credulity. As Vivian tells the paramour, being in love as opposed to merely loving requires acceding to the fiction of someone's "singular necessity"—the vestal's logic of *I can be happy only with you*. The paramour is too unreliable to have earned the tribute of that delusion. It's Vivian's puckish, passive-aggressive way of saying, "So far, you're not good enough."

"Ode on Indolence" is a caricature of detachment, a super-satirical striptease. It tries—not very hard—to contemplate the curious in-between of desire and skepticism, a somewhat disreputable zone that will be more familiar to some of us than others. It was not generally familiar to Keats, or it was not familiar to the Keats who is familiar to us from his no-holds-barred blitzes of epistolary passion, which seems unacquainted with the concept of going too far. If Vivian told Keats the same thing she tells the paramour—how could I let myself be in love with you, you're obviously completely untrust-worthy—he would no doubt have replied, as he did to Fanny Brawne on a Wednesday in June, 1820, "Be serious! Love is not a plaything—and again do not write unless you can do it with a crystal conscience."

That's the trouble with indolence: no one takes it seri-ously, but it is a serious behavior. In the seventeenth century the word came to mean "lethargy" or "inertia"; before that it meant "painless," in a doubled sense of giving and receiving no pain. To see indolence as easy living is entirely to mistake its anxieties and its grievances, for—if you ask *me*—the indolent person is bent crosswise by a craving she knows it is best to subdue. "Being in love," Vivian tells the paramour, is "a huge, beautiful luxury," and those who "do it with more facility" pay the highest cost. Or, as Jenny Von Westphalen wrote to her future husband, Karl Marx,

> What makes me miserable is that what would fill any other girl with inexpressible delight—your beautiful, touching, passion-ate love, the indescribably beautiful things you say about it, the inspiring creations of your imagination—all this only causes me anxiety and often reduces me to despair. The more I were to surrender myself to happiness, the more frightful would my fate be if your ardent love were to cease and you became cold and withdrawn.

If Keats told Jenny the same thing he tells Fanny—*be seri-ous and want what I want*—she might have replied as she did to Karl around 1839-40: "how little you know me, how little you appreciate my position, and how little you feel where my grief lies, where my heart bleeds."

Jenny's refuge is her own "hideous prose and mediocrity," stronger language than Vivian's wry detachment but hovering over the same button: press to exit. "Ode on Indolence" is not prose; it is, however, mediocre, which we might chalk up to nothing more complicated than the fact that indolence—the unassuming posture that regulates desperation through dullness, insensitivity, or a general attitude of no-big-deal—was not Keats's métier.

The nicest thing to say about the ode is that Keats is experimenting with a gentler key, to see if he can write without being, in Frank O'Hara's words, "emotionally hopped up or . . . self-excited." Two years before the composition of the odes, Keats found himself criticizing a painting for having "nothing to be intense upon, no woman one feels mad to kiss, no face swelling into reality." The ode takes these insufficiencies as its blueprint. It toys with detumescence as an aesthetic mode, as if Keats is trying to inhabit the indifference he so often projected upon the world and especially on Brawne. If the poem bombs, it is because he gives indifference no credit for affording others what he could never want for himself: a form of love that doesn't have to kill us even though it might.

What would it be like not to care? Keats was always curious about experiences that were not his own—that's the foundation of Negative Capability. In "Ode on Indolence," he tries apathy on for size. The result is a thin soup, for the poem can only imagine the avoidance of pain as a failure of nerve, or perhaps of character; indolence in *this* sense is cognate to the dream of mythic self-sufficiency that André Green associates with the "desire to kill" the beloved object in order to be free of its pull. This is the usual impulse behind not caring, and it's the same one that Keats, as we'll see, expresses near the ode's end: *I can't have it the way I want it so I don't want it at all* or, in the language of an amorous dictatorship, *I wanted you to love me but you didn't do it right*.

Looked at from a sympathetic angle, indolence is precisely what Barbara Browning imagines for Vivian and Jenny Von Westphalen for herself. It is not self-sufficiency but a complicated style of self-management, ideal for those who know their role in someone else's drama has half a dozen understudies. The indolent person is determined not to succumb to a Grand Guignol of insecurity and aggression, of the sort Vivian witnesses in a series of encounters with the paramour's exes, wives, or other lovers: the long-suffering girlfriend who dumps a wine glass full of Coke on Vivian's head, the young Greek woman who screams, "Bitch! Go back to America!" Indolence is the dream of not becoming a person like this. Indolence closes the heart like a fist and takes it on the chin, with the thought that it's better to choose a pain to weather now in order to avoid some much greater pain that lies inevitably down the line. But Keats misses this, the indolent person's pleasure in her own sly skill, which is its own form—inferior, quotidian—of genius. His poem would have been better if he had not.

*

If the ode is a striptease, it's the kind Barthes describes as a "meticulous exorcism of sex." That's surprising, because the mise-en-scène sets us up to expect a voluptuous daydream, a riffle through the erotic Rolodex. Lethargic and lounging, Keats is probably in bed, in a slow-start reverie that holds the day at arm's length. He is almost certainly in bed if we believe the account he included in a letter to his brother George and sister-in-law Georgiana, which is the basis for this poem:

This morning I am in a sort of temper indolent and supremely careless.... My passions are all asleep from my having slumbered from till nearly eleven and weakened the animal fibre all over me to a delightful sensation about three degrees on this side of faintness—if I had teeth of pearl and breath of lilies I should call it languor—but as I am[5] I must call it Laziness—In this state of effeminacy the fibres of the brain are relaxed in common with the rest of the body, and to such a happy degree that pleasure has no show of enticement and pain no unbearable frown. Neither Poetry, nor Ambition, nor Love have any alertness of countenance as they pass by me: they seem rather like three figures on a greek vase—a Man and two women—whom no one but myself could distinguish in their disguisement. This is the only happiness; and is a rare instance of advantage in the body overpowering the mind.

You will notice the association of indolence with compromised masculinity, the effeminacy of carelessness and poor muscle tone. Keep an eye on the man on the vase. This is no place for him and he will soon drop out.

The poem begins the same way. Three figures enter with "bowed necks" and, for a split second, on account of the epigraph, they might be the lilies of Luke or Matthew's field. But they have "joined hands" too, and faces, so they are people, though twice in five lines Keats calls them figures. He will also call them "shades" (once) and "shadows" (twice), "ghosts" and "phantoms," one a "maiden" and the other a "maid," for this is a poem strung on repetition of the least sophisticated kind.

The idea is that Keats is too lazy to think of better words or a greater variety of them. It's a dumbshow of indolence that extends to the verse, dominated, in this first stanza, by the voiced alveolar stop. Each line gets turned out with a thud, sometimes with several: bowed, joined, faced; behind, stepp'd; placid, san-

(5) Keats included a note: "because I have a black eye" from playing cricket the day before.

dals, graced; and so on along the tracks. The ode has the same respirating prosody as "Ode to a Nightingale" but with none of that poem's downy tread. These feet move slow but land hard.

The big question about this ode is whether it was written before or after the other ones. The similarities to "Grecian Urn" cut both ways: the urn could signal an early interest in classical imagery or a retrospective glance at what Keats had already achieved. Ditto "Ode to Psyche," whose beds of grass and casement windows also make an appearance, though in far less appealing circumstances than those given there. Then there is the question of its quality. Is "Ode on Indolence" as bad as it is because it was the first of the odes—the test drive, the dress rehearsal—or because it was the last, and Keats had run out of steam? The consensus that it *is* bad is universal, and it was the only one of the odes not published in Keats's lifetime (it saw daylight in 1848, the same year as *Vanity Fair* and *The Communist Manifesto*.)

There may be a smoking gun in the phrase "as may betide / With vases," a dry flourish that lands with another thud, this one somewhat leavened by self-mockery. *That's how it goes with vases, believe me I know.* The reference to Phidian lore is more convoluted, though it winks at another one of Keats's poems, the sonnet on the Elgin Marbles: Phidias is the Ancient Greek sculptor believed by some, including Keats's friend Benjamin Robert Haydon, to have created them. But why mention Phidias at all? Is the point here that someone who knows a lot about sculpture will come up short when faced with pottery, or else that expertise breeds confusion? Either way, the reference is dropped as soon as it's picked up, a free association that tenders nothing in the way of insight, because this is an exercise in low stakes. The speaker is spit-balling, thinking now of himself, now of his friends, now cracking a private joke. If something of the molten raptures of opium lingers in the second stanza—"Ripe was the drowsy hour. . . . my pulse grew less and less"— the poem's diction belongs to the more cogent exposition of the letter to George and Georgiana, and to the nonchalance of a mellower drug. "Kubla Khan" this is not.

Besides, there is no urn. The figures only move as if they are on one. This is a vision after all, not an ekphrasis, and the absence of anything concrete to look upon—any "alertness of countenance"—is another cue that this is Keats in the attempt of a very un-Keatsian frame of mind. No body can be truly in no pain; if we're not hurting now, we could be soon, or perhaps recently have been. And so, the poem takes as much leave as it can from *things*, fixing its gaze in the hazy never-been where pain could have "no sting, and pleasure's wreath no flower." The fantasy is not, as the speaker seems to suggest, of nothingness but rather of no consequences. Bobbing amid the no-risk equilibrium of idle days, pain is hypothetical, and pleasure comes with a cap; it will never bloom into the agonizing embrace of everything you have ever wanted nor will it fade and die. This is, perhaps, a good compromise.

Keats would not agree, but he has gotten this far and will see the experiment through. How does the indolent person, the prose-monger, the dopamine antagonist think? Apparently, in allegory. In the next half of the poem, the speaker is tormented, like Ebenezer Scrooge, by three spirits, here embodiments or, rather, essences of his greatest desires. As in the letter, they are Love, Ambition, and "Poesy," the archaic term introducing a note of discord or suspicion. Again, the poem is scrubbed of physical bodies, as if one of indolence's characteristic features were to see everything in the abstract—love divorced from lovers, ambition from goals, poesy from the roughening labor of poetics.

O'Hara says that thing about self-excitement in an essay on design, "the point where the poet can hold his ground in the impasse between formal smothering and emotional spilling over." Bow too low to the generic pressures of the ode and you lose the necessary friction between form and voice (personality, circumstance) that makes the poem distinct, this poem and no other; get too wrapped up in the thrill of precisifying your feelings and you have a poem that is at once over-composed and off-balance, a baked Alaska of mood.

When that happens, "the poet feels that his emotions are more important than any poem, that indeed they, not words *are* the poem." Design is how light and air get in. It is a set of visual, typographic, and subterranean cues that guide the poem through the white water of "half-thoughts, turgid emotions, secondhand insights, and all the rest, including a pat ending," and keep it from the gruesome fate of being predictable.

What to make of a poem like this one, which has so much design it is written *about* a design, organizing itself around a tableau vivant of negative vivacity? It is certainly not predictable, because we don't expect Keats to write like this, so flatly, with so loose a grip on the world of people and stuff. The poem lays design like a highway overpass over the muddy, mucky sands of love and sex and anger and despair that are Keats's usual stomping ground, and invites its three allegorical figures to go trundling over it. Each figure is sparsely bodied—an eyeball here, a sandal there—but no more than a saint on a stained-glass window, a jumble of tangents. Despite protests to the contrary, there is nothing about this trio that would make anyone burn or ache. They are tin men for the poem's tin ear.

Within the triplet, Love and Poesy make a pair. They are both young women, and Love, the fair Maid, extends her reach into the speaker's bond with Poesy, a "maiden most unmeek" whom Keats loves "more, the more of blame / Is heap'd upon her." There is perhaps a bit of the grim old virgin/whore dynamic being spun out here; maybe poetry is being asked to serve as the container or dumping-ground for appetites too frank to be directed elsewhere. If this is so, the speaker's insistence that he values poetry all the more for its absorption of blame tells us something new about that occult zone where pain has no sting and pleasure no flower—namely, that the poem could sometimes be that zone, the place where gratification goes to die.

Then there is Ambition, the sexless shape sandwiched between Poetry and Love. In his letter, Keats describes seeing Poetry, Ambition, and Love—in that order—as "a Man and two women." In the context of allegory, we might have expected "Love" to be the name of the god Cupid; it's Love that Cupid is called in "Ode to Psyche." We would have expected Poesy, with her connection to the Muses, to be female, and so she is. But Keats has done some scrambling. He's let Love be a Maid so she can stand in for a real person (Brawne), and he's made Ambition neither the Man nor the women of his eleven o'clock vision.

Nor, for that matter, is Ambition some potent form beyond the binary but an afterthought "it," a spurt that "springs / from a man's little heart's short fever-fit," that traffic jam of possessives squeezing Ambition right out of our mental picture. With chaste Love and unmeek Poesy already sent to opposite corners, the coy suggestion of group sex that floats around the opening stanza is by now completely quashed, and with it the last of the poem's imitation—never especially convincing—of vital force. What's left is a reminiscence of John Dryden's phrase "lambent dullness," the oxidizing flame that fuels a short drive to nowhere.

Keats has painted himself into a corner. On the one hand, we are meant to think that the appearance of these three phantoms is enough to set him ablaze. On the other, he has made his phantoms extremely phantasmatic, rough outlines of a concept or, more damningly, clichés. If Keats is testing himself, he realizes, about four lines into the fourth stanza, that he has absolutely failed, that the inhabitation of indolence for anything like an extended period of time is so foreign to him no amount of Negative Capability can help him pull it off.

What are the signs of this failure? The poem's repetitiousness is one; too many idles and masques by a half, and even "indolence" sounds twice. Its redundancies are another: "embroider'd" is close to "besprinkled" (more design), "shades" to "shadows." There are goofy, pseudo-Shakespearian interjections ("alas! wherefore?" "forsooth!" "O folly!") and awkward nominalizations ("annoy"), and verse so angular and ill-fitted it's sometimes hard to remember this is poetry at all.

I've said that this poem would have been better if it had contemplated indolence as a kind of love or as a theory of how to survive it. It would also have been a better poem if Keats had been able to contemplate indolence as a critical stance or, more radically, a utopian ideal. This might have been a poem about the abolition of work. Remember that Keats was alive during the first phase of the Industrial Revolution and saw the historical emergence of wage labor—in other terms, the rise of a society in which most people have to work in order to eat and so are forced to sell their labor power as a commodity, which is then put in service of generating profits for others. Keats was repelled by wage labor and its dirtier secret, the unwaged labor of the enslaved. By the nineteenth century, both were essential features of the world economy, which Keats excoriated in his poem *Isabella; or, the Pot of Basil.*

In *Isabella*, which George Bernard Shaw joked could have been written by Marx, Keats describes his heroine's evil brothers, a pair of merchants whose business, despite the poem's setting in Renaissance Italy, has a decidedly modern character:

> ... [F]or them many a weary hand did swelt
>   In torched mines and noisy factories,
> And many once proud-quiver'd loins did melt
>   In blood from stinging whip; —with hollow eyes
> Many all day in dazzling river stood,
> To take the rich-ored driftings of the flood.
>
> For them the Ceylon diver held his breath,
>   And went all naked to the hungry shark;
> For them his ears gush'd blood; for them in death
>   The seal on the cold ice with piteous bark
> Lay full of darts; for them alone did seethe
>   A thousand men in troubles wide and dark:
> Half-ignorant, they turn'd an easy wheel,
> That set sharp racks at work, to pinch and peel.

Scholars are accustomed to reading these lines for evidence of Keats's anti-capitalism. They serve that purpose well, not just because they make Isabella's brothers—Keats calls them "money-bags" and "ledger-men"—look bad, but because they make plain his own associations with *work*. This is not the amiable agricultural labor you'd find in georgic poetry or even in "To Autumn." This work happens in coal mines, assembly lines, and plantations. It is miserable and extremely dangerous, and it can require just as much cruelty from human beings as it dependably visits upon them.

From this vantage, Keats's opening epigraph—*they toil not, neither do they spin*—reads differently. It reads, that is, as the promise of a meaningful attack on the conditions of life circa 1819, and the expression of a better alternative that, for what it's worth, pops up not infrequently in the New Testament. If the poem had followed the promptings of its epigraph, it might have considered the *dolor* in *indolence* as a suffering indivisible from capital, as Alice Notley does when she populates a vision of hell with zombie like figures begging for "dolors" ("'I need a dolor' 'A few more dolors' 'Then after that' 'I'll see / our father.'")

Indolence in that case might have represented the desire to negate, cross out, or cancel the currency of that distinct historical pain; lounging in bed would not be just lounging in bed but declining to sell one's labor on the torture market, a more principled refusal than posting up "three degrees on this side of faintness." At the same time, this better, hypothetical poem would not apologize for loving laziness or its supple pleasures. It would celebrate sloth as the birthright of a human vigor emancipated from the requirement to make itself commercial. After the revolution, this poem would say, we will stretch out, in bodies new and strange and suddenly our own.

Again, this is not that poem. It certainly doesn't feature anything like *Isabella*'s critique of political economy. It is a very impersonal poem that clings nonetheless to the first person, while *Isabella* pointedly anonymizes the workforce against whose fate it rails. There, people are known synecdochally as parts—hands, loins, eyes, ears—in an eerie preapprehension of the "human brain[s], nerves, muscles, and sense organs" Marx sees vanish into the maw of the commodity. By the end of "Indolence," Keats is imagining a much blander diet. He tells his three phantoms he's not interested in being fed praise like "a pet lamb," even though they've offered nothing of the sort, and with that the poem effectively ends, since its last six lines do no more than iterate a single stiff demand.

Keats may not want to be that lamb, but since it's the only memorable image in the ode, he and we are stuck with it and its suggestion of inoffensive triviality. It's an old-timey image too, a pastoral hangover—a long way off from the torched mines and noisy factories into which indolence might have dropped like a bomb, like the anarchist demand Nanni Balestrini memorializes in the title of his novel *We Want Everything* and rephrases, more sharply, in its contents: "What the fuck did he care about it? He even said he wanted to help me: I'll find you another job, he said. No, you don't understand. I don't want to work anymore, I want to do nothing."

If time can be wasted, time must be precious. Reading this poem could be a bigger waste of time, but it also could have been a better one, lavish and free. Thanks, Keats, for the wrong nothing.

*

When he was dying, Keats decided he might like to be a lamb after all. "Yesterday and this morning," he wrote to Brawne, "I have been haunted with a sweet vision—I have seen you the whole time in your shepherdess dress." Who knows what she made of this? Keats was wrong to suspect Brawne didn't take things seriously. It's just that she had a comic way of marrying intensity to indifference, and had mastered detachment as a means of loving hard. In letters she sent to Keats's sister, mostly after his death, we see her warm to the small, silly trials of everyday life, the way they thrill in their very slightness, the way their slightness bears up a weight one hundred times its own measure.

"I am annoyed to death," she drawls, when an attempt to make purple dye from cochineal doesn't pan out; a careful and curious reader, she laughs at her own taste for "trumpery novels" and tells Fanny she mustn't try and test her memory on "whole verses or chapters . . . for though I can remember *pretty* well generally I read too many things to do so particularly—so what you may take for a proof of stupidity, is on the contrary through the great extensiveness of my studies."

Keats called her a flirt, and that's true. She laughed so much at herself, she assumed he might like to do the same, but instead he would crumple and then lash out, especially as he grew ill and flexed back to the primary primitive belief that he could not get love except by the backchannels of guilt and obligation. This is no criticism, since it is hard to be perfect and harder still to die. But still, let's take notice, however brief, of the special injustice done to the Fanny Brawnes of the world by the people they love, and who refuse to see their indolence— their mad belief in a love without fatalities, that might steer through difficulties without being sunk by them—as the passion it is. Nervous, doubting, and not without conditions, but passion nonetheless. In its way, it wants everything, and to work less for it.

Sources

Nanni Balestini. *We Want Everything*. Translated by Matt Holden. London: Verso, 2016.

Roland Barthes. *Mythologies*. Translated by Annette Lavers. New York: Farrar, Straus and Giroux, 1972.

Frances Brawne. Letter to Frances "Fanny" Keats [16 November 1823]. In *The Letters of Fanny Brawne to Fanny Keats, 1820–1824*. New York: Oxford University Press, 1937.

———. Letter to Fanny Keats [15 November 1821]. In Brawne, *Letters*.

Barbara Browning. *The Correspondence Artist*. New York: Two Dollar Radio, 2011.

John Dryden. *MacFlecknoe*. In *The Major Works*, edited by Keith Walker. Oxford: Oxford University Press, 2003.

André Green. *On Private Madness*. London: Routledge, 1996.

John Keats. *Isabella; or, the Pot of Basil*. In *Complete Poems*, edited by Jack Stillinger. Cambridge, MA: Harvard University Press, 1982.

———. Letter to Fanny Brawne, dated 5 July (?) 1820. In *The Letters of John Keats*, vol. 2, edited by Hyder Edward Rollins. 2 vols. Cambridge, MA: Harvard University Press, 1958.

———. Letter to George and Georgiana Keats, dated 14 February–3 May 1819. In Rollins, *Letters of John Keats*, vol. 2.

———. Letter to George and Tom Keats, dated 21, 27 (?) December 1817. In Rollins, *Letters of John Keats*, vol 1.

Karl Marx. *Capital*. Vol. 1. Translated by Ben Fowkes. London: Penguin, 1990.

Alice Notley. *The Descent of Alette*. New York: Penguin, 1996.

Frank O'Hara. "Design Etc." In *Standing Still and Walking in New York*. Bolinas: Grey Fox Press, 1975.

Jenny Von Westphalen. Letter to Karl Marx, dated 1839–40. In Karl Marx and Frederick Engels, *Collected Works*, vol. 1. New York: International Publishers, 1975.

Ode on Melancholy

No, no, go not to Lethe[1], neither twist
    Wolf's-bane, tight-rooted, for its poisonous wine;
Nor suffer thy pale forehead to be kiss'd
    By nightshade, ruby grape of Proserpine;
Make not your rosary of yew-berries,
      Nor let the beetle, nor the death-moth be
           Your mournful Psyche, nor the downy owl
A partner in your sorrow's mysteries;[2]
      For shade to shade will come too drowsily,
         And drown the wakeful anguish of the soul.

But when the melancholy fit shall fall
    Sudden from heaven like a weeping cloud,

(1) In Greek mythology, the river of forgetfulness (see "Ode on a Nightingale").
(2) The mystery religions of the ancient world were cults whose tenets were kept secret from everyone but their initiates, who underwent significant tests of faith before being let into the fold. The most famous are the Eleusinian Mysteries, which centered around the worship of mother-daughter goddesses Demeter and Persephone, or Proserpine. The story of Psyche is first told in Apuleius's second-century C.E. novel, *The Golden Ass,* parts of which seem to reflect a firsthand knowledge of mystery rituals.

That fosters the droop-headed flowers all,
    And hides the green hill in an April shroud;
Then glut thy sorrow on a morning rose,
      Or on the rainbow of the salt sand-wave,
        Or on the wealth of globed peonies;
Or if thy mistress some rich anger shows,
    Emprison her soft hand, and let her rave,
      And feed deep, deep upon her peerless eyes.

She dwells with Beauty—Beauty that must die;
    And Joy, whose hand is ever at his lips
Bidding adieu; and aching Pleasure nigh,
    Turning to poison while the bee-mouth sips:
Ay, in the very temple of Delight
    Veil'd Melancholy has her sovran shrine,
      Though seen of none save him whose strenuous
        tongue
    Can burst Joy's grape against his palate fine;
His soul shall taste the sadness of her might,
    And be among her cloudy trophies hung.

———

Here is the rare ode that begins by shutting down, or out. For that reason it is not very long, only three trim stanzas; it's an address in inverse, an uneasy conversation between a person and his problems. The Italian word *stanza* means room, and this poem has the rhythm of someone meandering about the house, from one room to another, loosening a string from his brain like Ariadne's thread in the Labyrinth of Crete. This is an apt comparison, since Keats's references to Prosperine, Psyche, and sorrow's mysteries invoke ancient rites of entrapment and liberation, death and rebirth, of which the story of

Theseus—who followed that thread right out of the maze—is also an allegory. "It is pretty generally suspected," Keats ventured, "that the christian scheme"—life after death—"has been copied . . . [from] hethen mythology." Shuffling around in itself, this poem thinks distantly of those stories and their happy promise. It does not, however, buy them.

No, no. "No" is a rhyme for "O" and also its negation; the poem will have nothing to praise. "No" is a half-rhyme for "thou" and offers it an ambivalent welcome: *not you again, in my head.* A stanza is not just a room but a station, a place to stand and take it. "Ecco qui / la stanza," writes Pasolini: "Here is the room,"

> *tomba dei tepori e delle*
> *tetre solitudini del mio corpo;*
> *lo specchio dove guardo, intenditore,*
> *gli scorci del mio viso; il letto senza*
> *fantasmi, nudo, a cui la nuda luce*
> *dá candori di gesso, e che il tuo riso*
> *sospende nel passato.*

> tomb of the warmths and
> dreary solitudes of my body;
> the mirror in which I observe, expertly,
> the pieces of my face; the bed without
> ghosts, naked, to which the naked light
> gives the whiteness of chalk, and your laugh
> suspends in the past.

You stand in a place until you can't stand it anymore. Lots of things can force you to move: any vexation or itch, a minor one that drives you into the kitchen for a glass of water, a larger one that launches you from the intolerable to the slightly less so. *No, no* is the sound of that movement: the first stanza opens at the closing of a door.

Melancholy is not mere sadness, nor is it the same as depression (all melancholies are depressions but not all depressions are melancholies). As Freud explains, melancholy arises from a trapped or uncompletable grieving that gets countered with an explosion of negative self-talk, a litany of "self-reproaches and self-revilings" whose job is to delay the final abdication of the lost object. As long as you keep talking or thinking or writing about what a failure and fraud you are, you hold off the disconsolate reality that this thing really is over, the lost object is lost, and it is—with a certain majestic inevitability— your fault. These are maladaptive behaviors, but they can be less painful than letting the person who's gone actually go. They are also a defense against rage, an inconvenient emotion melancholy channels into a "heightened self-criticism" that is, despite appearances to the contrary, the opposite of genuine self-awareness.

"In mourning it is the world which has become poor and empty; in melancholia it is the ego itself." The melancholy patient, says Freud, represents himself as "worthless, incapable of any achievement and morally despicable; he reproaches himself, vilifies himself and expects to be cast out and punished." The condition is given a false history: the patient maintains it was always thus, that he was never any better and shall never be different ("And I myself myself always to hate"—Thomas Wyatt). Melancholy is extravagantly long-winded: it likes to talk about itself, with an insistent communicativeness impervious to the thought that, just maybe, nobody wants to hear it. If melancholy has a genre, it is not the ode but the annotation.

For all its garrulousness, there is, as Keats says, a question mark hovering around melancholy, the conundrum of "sorrow's mysteries": we obviously get *something* out of suffering, since we so often elect to do it, but what? And why should being in love make melancholy's extreme existential pessimism even more seductive? Freud has an idea. Melancholy, he says, reveals the ambivalence built into all erotic relationships, the push-pull pathology of dread and longing, intimidation and tenderness we might as well call an "economics of pain." There is a kind of relief in bringing this contrariety into the open, in admitting that, as much as we say we don't like it, we keep going back for more. It's a curious feature of love that it convinces us to overvalue what we most resent: the demand that we put up more than we can stand to lose.

In Keats's ode, the economics of pain risks co-generating with the economics of boredom. Let's be clear: the push-pull game is a drag. Still, it is absorbing in the way of any tedium that seems about to break. That's why Keats, in his first ten lines, warns against using over-obvious symbols to express or extend the melancholy predicament but can't help himself from using them, too. These lines send up the canned phrases of Keats's earlier poems, in particular "Welcome joy, and welcome sorrow," which also begins with Lethe, the mythic stream of forgetfulness, and whose "Nightshade with the woodbine kissing" is carved up and repurposed in the command neither to twist wolf's-bane "Nor suffer thy pale forehead to be kiss'd / By nightshade." He knows better, and he doesn't.

In theory, the poem says, a good melancholy can't take the path of least resistance. It shouldn't pair dark moods with dark things—a "death-moth" or "downy owl"—because that will only take the edge off. The trick is to lay hold of the wakeful anguish of the soul and crack it even wider, crank it up, and this can only happen when melancholy rejects flimsy symbolism and roots itself in the real world. As always for Keats, the real world includes books, and "Ode on Melancholy" is a densely allusive poem with an obvious debt to a number of Renaissance texts, in particular Robert Burton's 1621 *Anatomy of Melan-choly*. It is also, and not coincidentally, preoccupied by gender, unsure of its exact role in pain's economy but convinced it must be close to central.

Under the sway of humoral theory, the early modern period viewed melancholy as an illness, the result of an overbalance of black bile (*melan-*, black; *kholē*, bile) that produced no fever but lots of drama. (Freud says that the melancholic's "complaints are really 'plaints' in the old sense of the word"— a musical lamentation or beating of the breast.) Over time, it became known as a psychosomatic condition that magnetized suffering to a noisy, ungovernable pleasure in distress. "Sorrow sticks by" melancholy people continually, wrote Burton, and no sooner

> are their eyes open, but after terrible and troublesome dreams their heavy hearts begin to sigh: they are fretting, chafing, sighing, grieving, complaining, finding faults, repining, grudging, weeping ... vexing themselves, disquieted in mind, with restless, unquiet thoughts, discontent, either for their own, other men's or public affairs, such as concern them not; things past, present, or to come, the remembrance of some disgrace, loss, injury, abuses &c. troubles them now being idle afresh, as if it were new done; they are afflicted otherwise for some danger, loss, want, shame, misery, that will certainly come, as they suspect and mistrust.... They can hardly be pleased or eased ... [Like] a deer that is struck, whether he run, go, rest with the herd, or alone, this grief remains: irresolution, inconstancy, vanity of mind, their fear, torture, care, jealousy, suspicion, &c., continues, and they cannot be relieved.

Keats captures the full-bore mania of Burton's prose when he calls it "a Feu de joie round the batteries of Fort St Hyphende-Phrase on the birthday of the Digamma," a great flaunting of words that is simultaneously savage, grandiloquent, and absurd—and for good reason. "I write," Burton admits, "of melancholy," and "by being busy to avoid" it.

In the eighteenth century, a bourgeois fad known as sentimentalism reclaimed melancholy as a moral stance. Sentimentalism socializes melancholy, highlighting its affinity for what Burton describes as an inflated sense of concern for other people's welfare. From it came poems like Thomas Warton's "The Pleasures of Melancholy" (1747), James Beattie's "The Triumph of Melancholy" (1760), and the complete works of the English Della Cruscans, all of which lick Burton's baggy, bad-feeling monster into a more convivial shape. At the end of Laurence Sterne's novel *A Sentimental Journey through France and Italy* (1768), the narrator comforts a woman by wiping her tears with his handkerchief; he then lets it "steep" in his own tears, then in hers, then in his again, overcome by feelings whose power can't be accounted for logically or traced to "any combinations of matter and motion."

Keats had a mixed opinion of this literature; "Ode on Indolence" ends with him scoffing at "sentimental farce." Still, he learned much from its premise that pain is an opportunity for intimacy and from its relentless emphasis on *fluid*. Sentimental literature is awash not just with tears but blushes, sweats, and other varieties of blood and mucus that subtilize the bile at melancholy's origin and make it polite, communicative: later editions of Henry Mackenzie's 1771 novel *The Man of Feeling* even came with an "index of tears" to help readers locate a favorite pitiful scene. In general Keats is tempted by liquidity, but this time he wants his melancholy muscular and rough. He wants, in Burton's words, the sorrow that sticks, the body that is struck—to inhabit the wound before it weeps.

And so when melancholy arrives like a weeping cloud it

must be met by something sturdier, with a better-bordered shape: "a morning rose," "a salt sand-wave," a peony, a hand. These are delicate objects but they all have a compactness or brevity of form, unlike the cloud whose motion is drawn out over four lines and several figures of speech ("But when the melancholy fit shall fall / Sudden from heaven like a weeping cloud, / That fosters the droop-headed flowers all, / And hides the green hill in an April shroud . . .") Those four lines—the second stanza's opening quartet—have the flavor of the first ten. They are self-consciously poetic, blunting the intensity of the melancholic fit. What follows has to erase them, and so the second half of this stanza delivers a series of terse edicts balanced on the rungs of six endstopped lines. "Glut" is the key word here: it means *choke on* or *swallow*, and the vulgarity here is no accident. It's arrived to call a halt to lyrical banalities and to introduce a more potent cliché: the singularly obnoxious, discouraging melancholy of heterosexual love.

Keats is not good at being macho, so he bootstraps his way there with help from a steadier meter and more confident rhymes: "cloud" and "shroud" instead of "owl" and "soul." Next to "glut" he sets the slightly archaic word "mistress," which anchors the boiler-plate pairing of exasperated woman—trembling with "some rich anger"—and doting yet dismissive man, here enjoined to "Emprison her soft hand, and let her rave, / And feed deep, deep upon her peerless eyes." *Mistress* means *lover*, but it's a word Wyatt or Shakespeare would use and Burton's *Anatomy* does, in a long memorable passage griping about how "Every Lover admires his Mistress, though she be very deformed of herself, ill-favored, wrinkled, pimpled, pale" and so on, which Keats copied out in full in a letter ("I would give my favou[r]ite leg," he explains, "to have written this as a speech in a Play"). They would also use this attitude, the dreamy condescension that treats women as a source of anxiety but can't imagine they might feel it, too.

The word "mistress" scores a couple of points. Because it is (unlike "lover") explicitly feminine, it suggests that gender is a fast track to melancholy's unsmiling pleasures. Because it is a bit dated or retro, it suggests that this way of imagining love—as stereotypically straight—is at once out of date and indestructible, as sturdy as the sonnet. Finally, because it is so powerfully literary in its associations, it implicates the ode and alas all poetry in an economics of pain that Freud could only begin to imagine and to which he may well have contributed: the dismal science of turning human beings into tropes, and love into a name for the disintegration of their potential.

All this is concentrated into one tidy allusion to *Paradise Lost*, which is, among other things, a poem about gender's invention and the possibility that *that* is our original sin. Consider Eve's account of her first meeting with Adam, and of how he scolded her when she tried, reasonably enough, to run away from him. It's an ugly memory strung across an ingenious enjambment, one that contradicts both Adam's version of events and the positive spin Eve has learned to give on them:

> With that thy gentle hand
> Seized mine: I yielded, and from that time see
> How beauty is excelled by manly grace
> And wisdom, which alone is truly fair.

Milton gives us "hand / seized" and Keats "emprison . . . hand"; both expose an iron fist in a velvet glove. The peerless eyes of Keats's mistress are Eve's eyes, their anger as inscrutable as what Milton calls her "meek surrender"—an obligatory pose of compliance hiding a resentment only Satan (and Milton's reader) can see. This is especially true if we're willing to hear the pun in "peerless," which implies not just that those eyes are without equal but also that they are hard to see into, trained, perhaps, on a distant fantasy of rebellion. "Peerless" might also mean that this mistress is not interested in looking back, that, faced with this tired programming, her attention has shuttered and gone dark.

Unlike *Paradise Lost*, Keats's poem doesn't have room for larger political or theological stakes. Its interests are much more narrow: how does an ode on melancholy make its subject present? It does it by swapping out the sterile poetic filigree of the first fourteen lines—a bow-legged sonnet stretched from stanza one to two—for a sexual misery that is recognizable and concrete, at once dumber and more terrible than any gothic bunting. *Do it this way*, the ode says, to really rip the eyelids off the wakeful anguish of the soul. "This feral malady," Burton calls it, with its "absurd and ridiculous tenets, and brain-sick positions." This theft of life, with its regressive promise; this confiscation of joy.

*

I was in the woods, and I hadn't gotten the memo. I wanted my melancholy atypical, nonconformist, kinky. In other words I didn't want any melancholy at all, but my circumstances made it impossible, because I had to share them with someone else. When we met this person looked at me, to borrow a description from Doris Lessing, with "the expert assessment of possibilities by a prisoner observing a new jailer." This was worrisome: it gave me the feeling that I was about to be played on an old but well-oiled machine, and besides, the last thing I wanted was to represent the impossibility of freedom, or to represent freedom at the expense of being free myself. Because I was ambivalent I collected reasons to remain so. Still, these would evaporate when held up next to my vague but no less stubborn belief that everything was going to be fine, in some moderately distant future that would be difficult to get to but worth it. What could I do? The worst seemed inevitable and the best necessary.

The upshot is that I wanted to be alone, and was lucky enough to have been invited where I could be: an island with a new and irrepressible urge to sink . There I go for a walk in the rain when it is too warm for November and get a thorn a little over a centimeter long stuck in the middle finger of my right hand, just above and to the left of my top knuckle. It goes completely underneath the skin and flattens into a dingy horizontal line. At first I try to ignore it, but by the time I get back to the place I am staying my finger is purple and enormous. I get on the internet and find what you might expect: wars and rumors of wars, the certainty of a bacterial infection, septicemia, and death.

All of this, by the way, is true. The island is a real place, the woods there are real, and I really did get a thorn stuck in my finger. None of this is written in code. I'm sorry I can't be more specific, won't use names or say the year, who was president, or how old I was. Honestly I'm not trying to be coy, just decent, since this is not only my story to tell. Every person I mention is a person with other people in what might be called the background of this writing, and that includes me—I am also a person with other people in the background of the intimacies that jump forward to become, even briefly, the whole of the world. A friend tells me he thinks that I think I'm laying my cards on the table when in fact I'm just being skittish and exasperating, that this is a chronic problem for me that I try to pass off as shyness but that he recognizes, because he recognizes it in himself, as evidence of a hard heart, loathe to leave itself unguarded. That hurts, but maybe he's right. Maybe what I imagine as discretion is just another way of trying to cut losses, to avoid the same risks I want others to take for me.

As the sky moves from black to gray and grayer, I am drenched in sweat with an arm on fire, mortified by self-pity. It has not escaped my attention that the thorn is absurdly on the nose, more death-moth than sand-wave. The air is still too warm as I travel onward to visit a friend (different friend) and help sterilize bottles for her breast milk. We turn on all the lights in her apartment and put on the Fall and Yusef Lateef, sing to her baby *all of it's bad, but it's not all bad*. Later I take a train to another city, where I see a friend (different friend) and argue with him, badly. I am glad of it now, my stupid wound, which feels comparatively clean and neat, and I am embarrassed by the force of my desire to have him touch absolutely nothing that is mine, certainly not the hand still pulsing with its vegetable stigma. "The resistance of the wood varies," warns Barthes, "depending on the place where we drive in the nail." In the last city everyone acts as though it's Christmas morning. I tell my hosts about the thorn and they take it so seriously I want to kiss them, in this delicate, disordered country where so much, it seems, is fatal.

Around this same time, I begin receiving messages from an old flame, who is in, for him, an unusual state of disinhibition. I would call it harassment, except that it's welcome; it has that quality of irritated insistence. He wants me to know I've ruined his life but he's always been like this, a great wet claw of hostility for whom spite is the sincerest proof of tenderness. He sends me digital photographs of ruined sidewalks, drugs, his face against a pillow. Soon we are trading lines from a Stephen Rodefer poem, a translation of François Villon that begins,

If the woman who I used to love
constantly and unconstantly

but who only wronged and hurt me,
finally fucking me over completely,
had only levelled with me from the start
and told me what she wanted (but no way)
I probably wouldn't have stayed with her.
I probably would have been free all this time.

It's fresh air—this person, this poem, this frankness—and now instead of globed peonies I am staring at a picture of his dick. All of this happens in the sidebar or perhaps the gutter of my melancholy; it is scar tissue growing around the thorn, burying its sticker. I am grateful for the way these obscenities steady me since, like Lauren Berlant, "there is nothing I like more than watching someone use their freedom." I am grateful, too, for their burlesque of the other love, for when the old flame vows to slap me and stuff my shirt into my mouth it loosens the secret of that relationship, at whose heart lies the radiant wish of two people to bear everything for each other but which has lately sagged into an actually degrading ritual of provocation and rebuke.

Once the jailer I'm now the object of an unflinching rhetoric of criminalization: everything I do is wrong. It comes easily to me to ask for forgiveness, but even though I really do mean it and really do want it I am also getting tired of this nonsense. If love is anything not laid waste by this world it is free. Mine is. Beneath all uncertainties it is sacred in the way of a riot, like the very idea of song. It has to be dragged kicking and screaming even from the scene of its final insult, for which I too am responsible, not least because I greet with furious exultation the moment it all goes to pieces and I abandon hope and us. From various corners I hear I have been characteristically insensible or clueless as well as hypocritical, beguiling, and cruel. No one seems convinced of what I know to be true about my love, that it was not wanted for what it was but for the pain it could guarantee.

Months later I will be out to dinner with two men, one of whom will tell a story about the time he lost his head over someone he describes as a mesmerizing nymphomaniac. The story turns on a dialogue with his analyst, whom he tries to persuade that women like this don't grow on trees. "For the men who need them," the analyst replies, "they do." We murmur and cluck over the exactness of this insight, congratulate one another on becoming adults no longer in thrall to our own worst impulses. Still I, who am not a nymphomaniac, cannot pretend the retort doesn't sting, that I don't hear it as a curse in the form of a question: what kind of woman am I?

*

Third and final room. There's confusion here, and it shows in the way the first half of the twenty-first line pauses on the threshold of the stanza before dragging itself forward. Who does "She" name? It seems, at first, that Keats is still talking about "thy mistress," as if her eyes and hand and anger have knit up into a person, anonymous but at least pronominal. But the accident of capitalization makes "She" seem bigger, mythic, and it turns out, by the stanza's end, that She is in part Melancholy herself, tricked out with a "sovran shrine" and "cloudy trophies" hung to dry.

Of course She is still the mistress, too, and this double meaning allows for yet another dip into the Petrarchan well where women are always allegorical. William Empson thinks the ode takes *mistress* and *Melancholy* as a single unit, in order to argue that only those who have first "achieved joy" through romantic love can appreciate the difficult grandeur of losing it. This wouldn't be an especially complex or original insight, and if it's true that "Ode on Melancholy" isn't Keats's most complex or original poem we might still want to give him a little more credit than that.

The ambiguity Empson picks up on here isn't rooted in a mix-up between joy and sorrow, but in melancholy's own instinct to convert the prospect of happiness into the certainty of defeat, even disaster. Most people assume those lines about bursting "Joy's grape" with a "strenuous tongue" are, like Keats's use of "glut," risqué, and that's true: they are meant to make you think of sex. But they are also, in a simpler sense, about wreckage, for under melancholy's sway sex is only ever an occasion for ruin or collapse. A burst is a pretty savage sort of explosion; a strenuous tongue doesn't just work hard, it works others too hard, too, and maybe this is also about language, about that insistent melancholic communicativeness that talks nonstop over its own impoverished imagination.

There is a mismatch between the way this poem begins and the way it ends. It begins by turning in on itself, with two emphatic negations. It ends, you might say, by flashing us: right in our faces it sets a very nearly pornographic metaphor of surfeit and catastrophe, satisfaction and damage. If the metaphor concerns joy it is also joyless, even harsh. Not for nothing does the last line—"And be among her cloudy trophies hung"—bring to mind Keats's famous ballad "La Belle Dame sans Merci," written around the same time as this ode. Neither poem can shake an idea of love as enslavement or captivity at which despair, "with horrid warning," gapes wide. Ultimately, then, the falling-back or retreat expressed by "No, no" and the acrid insult of the poem's finale add up to much the same thing: a grief that insists on being heard but refuses to be shared.

*

What about snow, or the memory of snow? In which room does it belong? Before the woods I wrote down the phrase "in my fantasies you pull the pleasure out of me like a thorn and I am finally empty, free." Now I admit I miss the endlessness of imagining us but not its terrors, and I make sure to hold those close. Every morning I touch my fear to make sure it's still there.

> If anybody asks me or wonders
> why I bad mouth love this way
> they'll have to figure it out for themselves.
> It's death that teaches you to speak of everything.

Sources

Roland Barthes. *A Lover's Discourse: Fragments*. Translated by Richard Howard. New York: Hill and Wang, 2001.

Lauren Berlant and Kathleen Stewart. *The Hundreds*. Durham, NC: Duke University Press, 2019.

Robert Burton. *The Anatomy of Melancholy*. New York: New York Review of Books Classics, 2001.

Jean Callais [Stephen Rodefer]. "Se celle." In *Villon*. Berkeley, CA: Pick Pocket, 1981.

William Empson. *Seven Types of Ambiguity*. New York: New Directions, 1947.

Sigmund Freud. "Mourning and Melancholia." In *The Standard Edition of the Complete Psychological Works of Sigmund Freud*, vol. 14, edited and translated by James Strachey. 24 vols. London: Hogarth Press, 1957.

John Keats. Letter to George and Georgiana Keats, dated 14 February–4 May 1819. In *The Letters of John Keats*, vol. 2, edited by Hyder Edward Rollins. 2 vols. Cambridge, MA: Harvard University Press, 1958.

———. "La Belle Dame sans Merci." In *Complete Poems*, edited by Jack Stillinger. Cambridge, MA: Harvard University Press, 1982.

———. "Welcome joy, and welcome sorrow." In Stillinger, *Complete Poems*.

Doris Lessing. *The Memoirs of a Survivor*. New York: Vintage, 1988.

Henry Mackenzie. *The Man of Feeling*. Oxford: Oxford University Press, 2009.

John Milton. *Paradise Lost*. In *Complete Poems and Major Prose*, edited by Merritt Y. Hughes. New York: Macmillan, 1957.

Pier Paolo Pasolini. *Dal Diario (1945–1947)*. Caltanissetta: Sciascia, 1954.

Laurence Sterne. *A Sentimental Journey through France and Italy*. New York: Penguin, 2002.

Thomas Wyatt. "The pillar perished is whereto I leant." In *The Complete Poems*, edited by R. A. Rebholz. London: Penguin, 1978.

Ode to Psyche

O Goddess! hear these tuneless numbers, wrung
    By sweet enforcement and remembrance dear,
And pardon that thy secrets should be sung
    Even into thine own soft-conched ear:
Surely I dreamt to-day, or did I see
    The winged Psyche[1] with awaken'd eyes?
I wander'd in a forest thoughtlessly,
    And, on the sudden, fainting with surprise,
Saw two fair creatures, couched side by side
    In deepest grass, beneath the whisp'ring roof
    Of leaves and trembled blossoms, where there ran
        A brooklet, scarce espied:
'Mid hush'd, cool-rooted flowers, fragrant-eyed,
    Blue, silver-white, and budded Tyrian[2],
They lay calm-breathing, on the bedded grass;
    Their arms embraced, and their pinions too;

---

(1) Psyche—the Greek word for "soul"—is a character from the second-century CE novel *The Golden Ass*. After a series of adventures, she becomes a goddess and the bride of Cupid or Eros, god of Love, who appears at the end of this first stanza as "the winged boy."
(2) Meaning "purple." Keats originally had "syrian;" his publisher made the substitution.

Their lips touch'd not, but had not bade adieu,
As if disjoined by soft-handed slumber,
And ready still past kisses to outnumber
    At tender eye-dawn of aurorean[3] love:
        The winged boy I knew;
But who wast thou, O happy, happy dove?
        His Psyche true!

O latest born and loveliest vision far
    Of all Olympus' faded hierarchy!
Fairer than Phoebe's sapphire-region'd star,
    Or Vesper, amorous glow-worm of the sky;[4]
Fairer than these, though temple thou hast none,
    Nor altar heap'd with flowers;
Nor virgin-choir to make delicious moan
    Upon the midnight hours;
No voice, no lute, no pipe, no incense sweet
    From chain-swung censer teeming;
No shrine, no grove, no oracle, no heat
    Of pale-mouth'd prophet dreaming.

O brightest! though too late for antique vows,
    Too, too late for the fond believing lyre,
When holy were the haunted forest boughs,
    Holy the air, the water, and the fire;
Yet even in these days so far retir'd
    From happy pieties, thy lucent fans,
    Fluttering among the faint Olympians,
I see, and sing, by my own eyes inspired.
So let me be thy choir, and make a moan

(3) Of the dawn, dawning.
(4) Phoebe is the goddess of the moon, which Keats calls her star. Vesper is the evening star.

Upon the midnight hours;
Thy voice, thy lute, thy pipe, thy incense sweet
From swinged censer teeming;
Thy shrine, thy grove, thy oracle, thy heat
Of pale-mouth'd prophet dreaming.

Yes, I will be thy priest, and build a fane[5]
In some untrodden region of my mind,
Where branched thoughts, new grown with pleasant pain,
Instead of pines shall murmur in the wind:
Far, far around shall those dark-cluster'd trees
Fledge the wild-ridged mountains steep by steep;
And there by zephyrs, streams, and birds, and bees,
The moss-lain Dryads shall be lull'd to sleep[6];
And in the midst of this wide quietness
A rosy sanctuary will I dress
With the wreath'd trellis of a working brain,
With buds, and bells, and stars without a name,
With all the gardener Fancy e'er could feign,
Who breeding flowers, will never breed the same:
And there shall be for thee all soft delight
That shadowy thought can win,
A bright torch, and a casement ope at night,
To let the warm Love[7] in!

———————

"Psyche" is an ode to joy. It takes the form of an epilogue or postscript to a story about desire, which is sometimes joy's ally and other times its antagonist. That story is the myth of Cupid

(5) A temple or shrine.
(6) A zephyr is a warm spring breeze; a dryad is a tree spirit.
(7) That is, Cupid (or Eros).

and Psyche, first told by the Numidian writer Apuleius in his second-century CE novel *The Golden Ass*. Psyche is a woman so beautiful that Venus, goddess of love, grows jealous, and orders her son Cupid to make her fall for someone worthless or, as she puts it, "extremus," the lowest of the low. By accident Cupid catches the sharp end of his own arrow and falls in love with Psyche himself; he then arranges for her to be brought to a magical palace where he can visit her in secret. Each night he makes love to Psyche without ever letting her see his face. It is, he tells her, for the best.

Keats knew *The Golden Ass,* but his primary inspiration came from Mary Tighe's 1805 *Psyche; or the Legend of Love,* an epic poem steeped in the concrete experience of femininity—it even opens with a sonnet to Tighe's mother. In an essay whimsically titled "When the Soul Had Hips," Herbert F. Tucker says Tighe's poem "is centered not on feminine desirability but on feminine desire," a claim borne out by its frank descriptions of Cupid's beauty: his cheeks are like "roses scattered o'er a bed of snow," his "polished limbs" are suffused with light, and so on. In her preface to *Psyche,* Tighe teases the "severe moralists" by reassuring them that, if they bother to read her long poem all the way through, they'll find only "innocent love, such as the purest bosom might confess." *Honi soit qui mal y pense.*

Tighe had been a favorite of Keats's when he was a teenager, and like most of us he looked back on his early loves with a mixture of bafflement and disdain. "I now see through" her, he told his brother and sister-in-law, "and can find nothing ... or weakness." "This same inadequacy," he adds, dogs women in general: "the Dress Maker, the blue Stocking and the most charming sentimentalist differ but in a Slight degree and are equally smokeable," meaning easy to see through, shallow. What Édouard Glissant so memorably terms "the right to opacity" is for Keats—or this version of him—a gendered prerogative. Men can retain their mystery even after a lengthy or intimate acquaintance; women, not so much.

The Greek word *psykhe* means "soul," and Psyche's myth is rightly understood as an allegory of personal moral development—the education of the soul as the seat of character and sensibility. It is also about the unequal distribution of secrecy, its pleasures, and its harms. If, as Keats thought, the world is less "a vale of tears" than a "vale of Soul-making" where "the heart must feel and suffer in a thousand diverse ways" before it can earn the exalted name of *soul*, the story of Psyche links suffering to sexual shame, and to the uniquely dispiriting ordeal of being kept secret or in the dark. He may try to wash his hands of her, but it's from Tighe that Keats learns to counter shame with sincerity, writing a poem of such sensual candor that it thoroughly debunks the tortured association of morality with abstinence. His ode is an effervescent, dead-serious challenge to the idea that "innocent love" is incompatible with carnal knowledge, or that the profane does not have an electric purity of its own.

Time passes, and Psyche gets pregnant. When her sisters come to visit, they put it into her head that her lover could be a demon or monster who's hiding his face while fattening her up for the kill. That night, Psyche waits until Cupid is asleep before creeping up on him with a dagger and lamp. She is shocked to discover the god of love, wings and all. "Between amazement, fear, and ecstasy," Tighe writes, she leans in for a closer look; a drop of oil from her lamp falls onto Cupid's shoulder, burning him. Cupid wakes up and, enraged, swoops out the window. Before he disappears, he treats Psyche to a stinging exit speech. He was, he gripes, trying to protect her, but she has ruined everything, and now he will punish her with his absence or retreat; in Latin the line is *"te . . . fuga mea puniuero."*

Te puniuero is a remarkable statement. It means not "you will be punished by" or "your punishment shall be" but "*I* will punish *you*." This is, undeniably, over the top. After all, it's Cupid who's created this horrible situation in the first place, and when Keats calls him "the winged boy" he's playing off an insight gleaned from Joseph Spence's 1747 *Polymetis*, a study of Greek and Roman myth and another old favorite.[8] To represent Cupid as a boy is to associate him not only with youth but with a certain insensitivity, even malice. One minute he is "very seriously employed about the catching of a butterfly," the next "intent to burn one with the torch he holds in his hand." This dual nature is suggestive: for the ancients, Spence explains, "a Cupid fondling or burning a butterfly" is just the same "as a Cupid caressing or tormenting the goddess Psyche, or the soul." This is a pun, sort of: *psyche* means soul but it also means "butterfly," hence Keats's reference to her "lucent fans" or wings.

This etymology makes good sense: what (as Spence says) could better demonstrate "the survival and liberty of the soul" than "an animal that is first a gross, heavy, creeping insect, and which, after dropping its slough, becomes, by an amazing change, a light, airy, flying, free, and happy creature"? Psyche will follow the same trajectory, but first she has to undergo a number of trials put together by Venus—to pass through what Keats calls the "World of Pains and troubles" necessary "to school an intelligence and make it a soul." The last of these involves a descent into Hell that Psyche nearly does not survive. In the nick of time Cupid, who has spent the meantime

(8) Keats's childhood friend Charles Cowden Clarke lists *Polymetis*, with *Tooke's Pantheon of the Heathen Gods and Illustrious Heroes* and John Lemprière's *Bibliotheca Classica*, among the books that were "constantly recurrent sources of attraction" for the young poet.

imprisoned in his mother's house, slips out of an open window and hustles to her side. In Tighe's account of their reunion, the lovers are like two candles, which

> with pure converging rays,
> In momentary flash their beams unite,
> Shedding but one inseparable blaze
> Of blended radiance and effulgence bright,
> Self-lost in mutual intermingling light;
> Thus, in her lover's circling arms embraced,
> The fainting Psyche's soul, by sudden flight,
> With his its subtlest essence interlaced;
> Oh! bliss too vast for thought! by words how poorly traced!

"Self-lost"—you can see why Keats used to love this poem. Everything ends well: Venus throws in the towel, Psyche is made immortal and gives birth to a daughter, whose name is Pleasure.

*

Keats sets his ode in the aftermath of all this drama. On the one hand, this lets him sidestep the questions about gender and power that both the original text and Tighe raise. On the other, it helps him write a poem rich in utopian impulses, including the near-total annulment of gender itself. There is a lone masculine possessive in the twenty-third line ("His Psyche true!") but the lovers are otherwise afloat in a euphoria of third-person plurals: "they lay calm-breathing," "their arms," "their pinions," "their lips." A line like "Two fair creatures, couched side by side" likewise conveys plural life within a singular form. They are side by side but they are not the same; they are different, but their difference can't be parsed pronominally, by words like "him" or "her." They are divine but they are also just bodies or, you might say, free.

So much of this poem is about leaving things behind—about the disappearance of what cannot be brought with us into a future of perfect love. Even if Keats won't say so, he is indebted to Psyche's trip into Hell as a blueprint for this kind of renunciation. The descent into the underworld is a familiar trope from classical mythology, especially in stories about goddesses; Psyche is just one in a long line of ancient heroines who prove their magnanimity (literally, their greatness of soul) by being willing to lose everything, including their lives. In the Sumerian poem *The Descent of Inanna*, the titular goddess passes through a series of subterranean gates, removing a piece of clothing or jewelry at each one until she arrives naked at the throne of her sister Ereshkigal, where she is promptly "turned into a corpse, / A piece of rotting meat / And . . . hung from a hook in the wall."

The Descent of Inanna is one of Alice Notley's source texts for her 1996 poem *The Descent of Alette*, which, like Tighe's *Psyche*, defines itself explicitly as "a feminine epic." Moving through a nightmarish underground landscape, Alette is on a mission to assassinate a seemingly omnipotent male power known only as "the tyrant,"

> "a man in charge of" "the fact" "that we were"
> "below the ground" "endlessly riding" "our trains, never
>   surfacing"
> "A man who" "would make you pay" "so much" "to leave the
>   subway"
>
> "that you don't" "ever ask" "how much it is" "It is, in effect,"
> "all of you, & more" "Most of which you already" "pay to

live below" "But he would literally" "take your soul"
    "Which is
what you are" "below the ground"

In a sense, Notley explains elsewhere, "the tyrant is us." He is "the form of our life, the form of our politics, the form of our universities, the form of our knowledge, our thinking we know something." All these forms, she adds, have been responsible for exiling feminized subjects from the public sphere—for keeping them, you might say, in the dark. "We were banished," says Notley, "and so we became the psyche," the untamed inner prompting that does not accept this state of affairs, that asks for more even as its yearning is punished and forsaken.

"Ode to Psyche" is out to vanquish these forms and find out what else there might be. It is a love poem crossed with a social critique. That much is evident in its tiptoeing away from the gender binary, and it is even more apparent in its treatment of religion, which Keats associates with two of his least favorite things: social inequality and compulsory abstinence. When Keats says that Psyche is "too late" for them—too late to be counted among the "faded hierarchy" of the Olympian gods, too late to be worshiped by a "virgin-choir"—he means it as a compliment and as a gift. Because she is not an ancient goddess like Inanna but a newly minted one (it's entirely possible Apuleius made her up), Psyche gets to stand for the usurpation or even the eradication of the older, crueler, and more autocratic order to which both her lover and his mother belong. In other words, Psyche's belatedness allows Keats to go after Notley's targets: institutions that have historically constrained what it's possible for us to do and be.

One of Keats's earliest poems was a sonnet called "Written in Disgust of Vulgar Superstition," which rolls its eyes at "the sermon's horrid sounds" and the "outburnt lamp" of religious orthodoxy. The poem ends by promising a windfall of "fresh flowers" and "many glories of immortal stamp" to replace them, setting the endlessly regenerating beauties of nature and the imperishable beauties of art against the ugly, unforgiving world of "church bells," cults, and creeds. "Ode to Psyche" resurrects these tropes, from the instruments of church ritual—voice, lute, pipe, "incense sweet/From chain-swung censer teeming"—to the flowers that Fancy, or the imagination, supplies in their stead.

This is a political takeover as well as a secular one, as that line about "Olympus' faded hierarchy" might suggest. Like the ode's anti-clerical sentiment, this phrase signals a certain subtle affinity for the principles of the French Revolution, which abolished feudalism and effectively outlawed the Catholic Church. In his letters Keats defends the Revolution even given its violent turn; he also maintains that England needs a mass uprising of its own. In this poem, he roots loudly for the obsolescence of hierarchies of all kinds, implicitly countering their top-down format with the equitable side-by-sideness of Cupid and Psyche's embrace. A couple is not a revolutionary society, to be sure. It is, nonetheless, the model Keats gives of a communal existence set loose from any imposition except the "sweet enforcement" of appetite and ardor.

Here's a surprise: Keats also commits *himself* to extinction. He wants a world made out of poems, not personalities, which is why by the ode's end he has reduced his own presence merely to "the wreath'd trellis of a working brain" and the "branched thoughts" scrabbling over them. The suggestion of latticework here mimics the folds of the cerebral cortex, so that the poem becomes a memento mori in reverse: instead of an arid, empty skull we get a pulsing, vital organ. It's a classic Keatsian image—carnal with more than a flicker of the grotesque—and it reminds us not to dread but rather to hope, actively and passionately, for our lives to be low-impact or, if you like, biodegradable. That wish is set to music by the ode's final stanza, with its tender collection of hisses (*moss, midst, quietness, dress, trellis*) and half-muted moans (*murmur, zephyr, lull*) atomized against the air.

Nothing good has ever come out of civilization except this: the dream of its end. This isn't a nihilistic poem but it is a radical one, with a strong ecological undercurrent. It suggests that the only kind of world in which real love is possible is a world in which people are liberated by their own fragility, where they can approach the condition of trees, flowers, stars, and sounds and abandon the lamentable fantasy of leaving their mark on the world or each other. Keats says as much in "Sleep and Poetry," an otherwise insipid poem from 1816 that anticipates the vision with which the ode begins. There, Keats and his lover find themselves "in the bosom of a leafy world" where they "rest in silence, like two gems upcurl'd / In the recesses of a pearly shell." This is where Keats finds Cupid and Psyche, too, in a gentle parenthesis between the difficulties of the past and the "wide quietness" of the future—the open end where anything, finally, could happen.

There is more to say about that word "branched," as in "branched thoughts." When Cupid is scolding his bride he calls her "Simplicissima Psyche": the simplest, the most naive. It's an unreasonable adjective (again, whose fault is this anyway?) but it suits Apuleius's purpose, which Keats shares. That purpose is to argue that suffering, in making us less simple, makes us worthy of love—not in some narrow masochistic sense, but because suffering gives us access to communal existence, the life we share with others by virtue of being alive at all. Maybe it's a coincidence, but maybe it means something that *simplicissima* is also a technical term from botany meaning "without any branches" or, more simply, unbranched.

Keats was interested in botany, and it's tempting to think

he knew the scientific import of *simplicissima*, since he uses its inverse so beautifully to convey the soul's metamorphosis from impulsive innocence to well-traveled maturity. *Branched* is a metaphor of expansion and connection, of growth that comes only from an acquaintance with pain, "pleasant" or otherwise. The figure's organic character fits with the larger argument or attitude of the poem, which so desperately wants to imagine an existence free to be brief, even frail. That is why this poem ends with a scene of infinite receptivity, as Keats imagines propping open a window "to let the warm Love"—that is, Cupid—"in." This is a promise of sex to be sure, but it is also a promise to remain unguarded, even to the possibility that barely makes a sound.

*

What is it that Psyche is after, and why is she punished? That's easy: she wants to see the body of the person she loves. For Cupid, this desire is *simplicissima*: sophomoric, unseasoned, lacking in perspective. "O simple Psyches," he wails in William Adlington's 1566 translation, "consider with thy selfe how I, little regarding the commandement of my mother (who willed mee that thou shouldst be married to a man of base and miserable condition) did come my selfe from heaven to love thee, and wounded myne owne body with my proper weapons, to have thee to my Spowse." For Psyche, it is the basis of the exact same form of liberation Keats gives her in his first two stanzas. She wants to fast-forward to precisely that moment, to cut to the feeling of being self-lost in honest passion.

This emphasis on Psyche's desire separates Apuleius's story from its best-known adaptation, *La Belle et La Bête* (*Beauty and the Beast*), first published in 1740 by the French novelist Gabrielle-Suzanne Barbot de Villeneuve. All the key elements are there—the jealous sisters, the enchanted palace manned by invisible servants ("*solas voces famulas habebat,*" says Apuleius: "she had nothing but voices for handmaids"), the threat of an inhuman, possibly monstrous mate—with one glaring exception. The tale of Beauty, as everyone from Bruno Bettelheim to Jean Cocteau to Marina Warner to Angela Carter understands, is about the fear of adult sexuality cast as a pas de deux between male appetite and female repulsion. The tale of Psyche is about a person's refusal to be less than human and the god who feels it like a wound.

As far as Cupid is concerned, his arrangement with Psyche has everything, including the triple allure of infidelity (he betrays Venus), valor (but only to protect Psyche), and self-congratulation (all at his own expense). And yet he doesn't mean to be sleazy or cruel. He is part of the allegory too, though Dorothy Van Ghent seems to have the deep truth of it backwards when she says Cupid represents "the darkness of primal instinct" and Psyche "the 'soul's' distrust of the sensual." On the contrary, it is her curiosity that throws him for a loop and his bad faith that lets her down. "Did I seem a beast unto thee," Cupid demands, "that thou shouldst go about to cut off my head with a razor, who loved thee so well?" Of course not. The real fear in play is that the winged boy is the monster she's been promised, not because he is a beast but because he is a child.

Then again, maybe Psyche didn't care if her lover was a monster; maybe she had things to say that couldn't be said in the dark, and was tired of speaking like someone who does not want to be heard. Keats is on her side, so he opens, closes, and generally overloads his ode with images of light and sight. "Surely I dreamt *to-day,*" he says, instantly opposing this scene to the nights of stealth and masquerade that have preceded it. The whole first stanza describes an act of vision that is positively visionary—Keats's eyes aren't just open but "awaken'd"—and in the second he imagines Cupid and Psyche waking up next to each other as an "eye-dawn," a sleepy revelation. Originally "O brightest!" was "O bloomiest" until Keats or maybe his editors had the good sense to change it and give Psyche exactly the name she deserves, one that closes the distance between her victory and her crime.

Cupid, you may remember, reunites with Psyche after escaping his mother's house through an open window. At the end of Keats's ode, he comes to her via a "casement ope." It's a shrewd callback by Keats, who wants us to know that Love has suffered too, been hurt and held captive and found his own way out. Thus this final image of illumination and clearing is also an acknowledgment of shared effort, and that tells us something new. The ode is an allegory of the soul's refinement, and of what Wordsworth called the growth of a poet's mind; it is an allegory about the end of culture, and how things would be better if we had fewer things (Notley: "I think people should be that way—they shouldn't have any money, and they should talk a lot"). But "Ode to Psyche" is also a piece of advice about intimacy: the soul can't rescue love, but it can make room for love to arrive even in the wake of a great and reciprocal betrayal. This is more of a wish than a guarantee. It is nonetheless dearly meant, and merciful, and kind.

*

Keats's kindness is the great secret of the odes, if we understand *kind* as Shakespeare does, to mean something irreducibly connected to human nature—to, that is, our kind. Walter Jackson Bate, not actually a fan of this poem, says its principal interest lies in "that, through writing it, Keats learned better how to proceed." You don't have to agree with the faintness of this praise to believe that "Psyche" is the skeleton key to the odes or, really, to Keats's entire poetic project.

In the introduction to this book, I suggested that Keats wants to capture in poetry the same suite of effects Marx will attribute to the abolition of private property. Under those happy circumstances, we would not only experience "the complete emancipation of all human senses and attributes" but also their socialization, the synthesis of human nature with social being. "The senses and enjoyments of other men," writes Marx, will become available to me as my own senses and enjoyments, and my relationships with others "an organ for expressing my own life." All the odes rehearse this dream, and "Psyche" does it in the most straightforward way possible, by imagining sexual love—adult, consensual, private but not secret, without shame but not without principles—as the emancipation of the self in the body of another. This is what Mariarosa Dalla Costa means when she calls sexuality "the most social of expressions"; like love it is, at its best, a form of kindness that makes good on what we are, conveying us if only for moments at a time to our shared essential destiny.

On one side of Psyche, then, lie those primordial myths of descent and ascension, abandonment and recovery. On her other side, the modern dream of a form of emancipatory relation in which, Marx says, "the eye has become a *human* eye, just as its *object* has become a social, *human* object—an object emanating from man for man." Both aspects of the goddess's story are folded into that image of her and Cupid definitively side by side, in precisely such a posture of sensuous interdependence. The image is a shorthand intended to convey what it would be impossible to know in advance: how things might be otherwise in this browbeaten world, which, despite everything, somehow "fails to feel its own incompleteness." Some would say that love is the mood of that incompleteness, its limited compensatory gesture. Others, like Keats, would say love is its defiance.

There is another Sumerian poem about Inanna, called *The Courtship of Inanna and Dumuzi*. It is sometimes referred to as the world's first love story and was an early template for the Song of Songs. After some disdainful hemming and hawing, the goddess takes the shepherd Dumuzi as her lover; like the marriage of Cupid and Psyche, this courtship involves an apotheosis, through which Dumuzi becomes a god and king. In sinuous passages alternating call with response, the poem celebrates their union in language at once (in the words of its translator) "tender, erotic, shocking, and compassionate." The lovers use a ritual script that has the quality of spontaneous, intimate utterance, while their words of obscene praise and command have the gravity of a sacred text: "Your broad field pours out plants./Your broad field pours out grain . . . Pour it out for me, Inanna./I will drink all you offer." In the dead middle of all this comes the same parenthesis or breathing space around which Keats builds his ode:

> He put his hand in her hand.
> He put his hand to her heart.
> Sweet is the sleep of hand-to-hand.
> Sweeter still is the sleep of heart-to-heart.

This is a good dream; they all were.

Sources

William Adlington. *The Golden Ass of Apuleius*. London: John Lehmann, 1946.

Apuleius. *Cupid and Psyche*. Edited by E. J. Kenney. Cambridge: Cambridge University Press, 1991.

Charles and Mary Cowden Clarke. *Recollections of Writers*. London: Sampson Low, Marston, Searle, & Rivington, 1878.

Mariarosa Dalla Costa. "Women and the Subversion of the Community." In *Women and the Subversion of the Community: A Mariarosa Dalla Costa Reader*, edited by Camille Barbagallo. Oakland: PM Press, 2019.

Édouard Glissant. *Poetics of Relation*. Translated by Betsy Wing. Ann Arbor: University of Michigan Press, 1997.

John Keats. "Written in Disgust of Vulgar Superstition." In *Complete Poems*, edited by Jack Stillinger. Cambridge, MA: Harvard University Press, 1982.

———. Letter to George and Georgiana Keats, dated 31 December 1818. In *The Letters of John Keats*, vol. 1, edited by Hyder Edward Rollins. 2 vols. Cambridge, MA: Harvard University Press, 1958.

Karl Marx. [Private Property and Communism. Various Stages of Development of Communist Views. Crude, Equalitarian Communism and Communism as Socialism Coinciding with Humaneness]. In *Economic and Philosophic Manuscripts of 1844*, translated by Martin Milligan. Amherst, NY: Prometheus Books, 1988.

Alice Notley. *The Descent of Alette*. New York: Penguin, 1996.

——— and Shoshana Olidort. "Between the Living and the Dead: An Interview with Alice Notley." *Los Angeles Review of Books*, 25 December 2016.

Joseph Spence. *Polymetis; or, an Enquiry Concerning the Agreement between the Works of the Roman poets, and the Remains of the Antient Artists. Being an Attempt to Illustrate Them Mutually from One Another*. London: R. Dodsley, 1747.

Mary Tighe. *Psyche; or, the Legend of Love*. In *The Collected Poems and*

Journals of Mary Tighe, edited by Harriet Kramer Linkin. Lexington: University Press of Kentucky, 2005.

Herbert F. Tucker. "When the Soul Had Hips: Six Animadversions on Psyche and Gender in Nineteenth-Century Poetry." In *Sexualities in Victorian Britain*, edited by Andrew H. Miller and James Eli Adams. Bloomington: Indiana University Press, 1996.

Dorothy Van Ghent. *Keats: The Myth of the Hero*. Revised and edited by Jeffrey Cane Robinson. Princeton, NJ: Princeton University Press, 1983.

Diane Wolkstein and Samuel Noah Kramer. *Inanna, Queen of Heaven and Earth. Her Stories and Hymns from Sumer*. New York: Harper Perennial, 1983.

To Autumn

Season of mists and mellow fruitfulness,
    Close bosom-friend of the maturing sun;
Conspiring with him how to load and bless
    With fruit the vines that round the thatch-eves run;
To bend with apples the moss'd cottage-trees,
    And fill all fruit with ripeness to the core;
        To swell the gourd, and plump the hazel shells
    With a sweet kernel; to set budding more,
And still more, later flowers for the bees,
Until they think warm days will never cease,
        For summer has o'er-brimm'd their clammy cells.

Who hath not seen thee oft amid thy store?
    Sometimes whoever seeks abroad may find
Thee sitting careless on a granary[1] floor,
    Thy hair soft-lifted by the winnowing wind;
Or on a half-reap'd furrow sound asleep,
    Drows'd with the fume of poppies, while thy hook
        Spares the next swath and all its twined flowers:
And sometimes like a gleaner thou dost keep

(1) A storehouse for threshed grain.

Steady thy laden head across a brook;
   Or by a cyder-press, with patient look,
      Thou watchest the last oozings hours by hours.

Where are the songs of spring? Ay, where are they?
   Think not of them, thou hast thy music too,—
While barred clouds bloom the soft-dying day,
   And touch the stubble-plains with rosy hue;
Then in a wailful choir the small gnats mourn
   Among the river sallows, borne aloft
      Or sinking as the light wind lives or dies;
And full-grown lambs loud bleat from hilly bourn;
   Hedge-crickets sing; and now with treble soft
   The red-breast whistles from a garden-croft;
      And gathering swallows twitter in the skies.

———————

there are those who can tell you
how to make molotov cocktails, flamethrowers,
bombs whatever
you might be needing
find them and learn, define
your aim clearly, choose your ammo
with that in mind

*

"To Autumn" is perfect and unforgivable. It is the most definitively dated of all the odes, written on September 19, 1819. We know this because Keats told a friend about the circumstances of its composition, which took place during a writing retreat in Winchester:

How beautiful the season is now—How fine the air. A temperate sharpness about it. Really, without joking, chaste weather—Dian skies—I never liked stubble-fields so much as now—Aye better than the chilly green of the Spring. Somehow, a stubble-field looks warm—in the same way that some pictures look warm. This struck me so much in my Sunday's walk that I composed upon it.

So much of the poem is here, down to the exclamatory "Aye" that ushers in a comparison between Autumn and Spring, in which Autumn comes out on top. "Chaste" is a funny word to use and Keats knows it; he says he's not joking but then he immediately makes a joke, calling the sky "Dian" after Diana, the virgin goddess of the hunt, his nerdiness compulsive and droll as always. Diana will reappear in the ode, dropped down from heaven to earth and shimmied into the ungendered figure of Autumn itself, her chastity recast as a more Keatsian voluptuousness that is also—and this is Keatsian, too—filmier and faint.

Why unforgivable? As he sat tucked up in Winchester, Keats read a horrific report in the papers. Just four weeks earlier, on August 16, a crowd of between sixty and eighty thousand people had assembled for a peaceful demonstration at St. Peter's Field, Manchester; a number of activists, including the political celebrity Henry Hunt, were slated to speak. The local magistrates had put together a large security force that included the Manchester and Salford Yeomanry, a volunteer regiment of landowners and merchants with its origins in wartime militia movements. Since 1817, in response to a series of riots, the Yeomanry had taken up the cause of suppressing unrest among Manchester's working class, hard-hit by the economic depression that followed the Napoleonic Wars. Around 1:30 p.m., the magistrates decided to have Hunt arrested. As the regiments rode in, a mounted trooper struck Ann Fildes with his horse, so hard that her two-year-old son William, whom she was carrying in her arms, flew two and a half yards out in front of her and broke his head open on the street.

William Fildes was the first casualty of what would come to be known as the Peterloo Massacre. By 1:35 p.m. the cavalry had charged into the crowd, sabers drawn and slashing indiscriminately; people ran for the walls enclosing the field, and so many fell and were trampled that their bodies quickly piled up into large heaps. In his memoir *Passages in the Life of a Radical*, Samuel Bamford would recall a trigger-happy cavalry cutting "through naked held-up hands and defenceless heads," "dashing whenever there was an opening," "pressing and wounding" and a terrified crowd screaming, "'Break! break! they are killing them in front, and they cannot get away.'" Separated in the crush from her husband, Jemima Bamford ducked into the cellar of a nearby residence, where she could hear both "the cries of the multitude" and the family upstairs— "bewailing most pitifully"—as they reacted to what was happening outside:

> They could see all the dreadful work through the window, and their exclamations were so distressing, that I put my fingers in my ears to prevent my hearing more; and on removing them, I understood that a young man had just been brought past, wounded. The front door of the passage before mentioned, soon after opened, and a number of men entered, carrying the body of a decent, middle-aged woman, who had been killed. I thought they were going to put her beside me, and was about to scream, but they took her forward, and deposited her in some premises at the back of the house.

By 1:45 p.m. there were, by official count, 650 wounded and fifteen dead. The latter category includes John Ashton, who had been carrying the flag of his trade union; seventeen-year-old William Bradshaw, shot by a musket; brothers William and Edmund Dawson; and Mary Heys, a pregnant mother of six who was trampled so severely that she had seizures right up until she delivered her baby two months early, and died just before Christmas.

"You will hear by the papers of the proceedings at Manchester," Keats writes to his brother on September 18, the day before he would compose his ode. No more is said, and several paragraphs later, he makes an unfortunate crack about having "struck for wages, like the Manchester weavers" to drive up the price of his puns. It's true that, just before his remark about Peterloo, Keats has been going on at length about the political climate, noting that the "unlucky termination" of the French Revolution had allowed the British state to "spread a horrid superstition against all innovation and improvement" and thus "to undermine our freedom." It's also true—and this is important—that he defines "the present struggle in England of the people" as the destruction of that superstition and the insistence on moving forward at all costs.

When he mentions Peterloo, however, it is to explain why he thinks the state won't prosecute a radical publisher named Richard Carlile for sedition, despite the fact that, since the 1790s, a succession of Tory governments had more or less declared open war on the free press. Just look, Keats says, how much the people love Henry Hunt, whose return to London from Manchester was greeted by some thirty thousand well-wishers.

In short, Peterloo does not appear to have stopped Keats's world on its axis. He seems to have been fairly unusual in that regard. At the time, even non-partisan newspapers reflected a deeply felt astonishment that Englishmen would kill their own unarmed people, while conservative and left-leaning journalists alike trumpeted Peterloo as the loudest if not the first shot in an intensifying class war. This is exactly how it appeared to Percy Bysshe Shelley, whose incendiary ballad, "The Mask of Anarchy," is often invoked as the anti–"To Autumn" and used to put it to shame.

Shelley's poem advertises itself as a prophetic dream or vision, in which Shelley (who was living in Italy) sees the events of Peterloo unfold as a *mask*, a pantomime or play. The anthropomorphic figures of Murder, Fraud, Hypocrisy, and of course Anarchy—which, in Shelley's usage, means lawless or illegitimate government and not the absence of government altogether—ride by in a diabolical parade. Soon, on Anarchy's orders, his troops begin to attack the crowd, which is made up of those who ply the "loom, and plough, and sword, and spade," which is to say the working class. But then Hope appears, a "maniac maid" who, somewhat shockingly, enjoins the crowd to nonviolent resistance: "Let them ride among you there, / Slash, and stab, and maim, and hew,— / What they like, that let them do." Her argument is simple, and she makes a simple promise:

> . . . that slaughter to the Nation
> Shall steam up like inspiration,
> Eloquent, oracular;
> A volcano heard afar.

The death and maiming of the innocent, in other words, will make a big impression on those who remain alive, and they in turn will "Rise like Lions after slumber / In unvanquishable number." The poem concludes with what has become its best-known line: "Ye are many—they are few."

"The Mask of Anarchy" is a messy, spectacular performance, all the more powerful for its glitches—its erratic meter and punctuation, its lurid images, its gonzo cast of real and allegorical characters—which announce with total conviction the necessity of subordinating conventional ideas of poetic beauty to something even more beautiful and even more necessary: in a word, revolution. Slapped down next to it, Keats's ode cuts an awkward if not outright hideous figure, so intrusively lovely thirty-four days out from a high-profile human disaster. It *is* perfect, which means it needs nothing. "The Mask of Anarchy," with its angry, insistent address, dares to need us all. It is a love poem in the way Juliana Spahr means when she invokes "art that has a crowd scene in it in which the crowd has been loved." It is a love poem, too, because it asks for so much, none of it for itself.

*

it is not a good idea to tote a gun
or a knife
unless you are proficient in its use
all swords are two-edged, can be used against you
by anyone who can get 'em away from you

*

Keats scholars, of course, will bend over backwards to tell you that "To Autumn" is about Peterloo and, by tortuous extension, the revolution. This is partly in response to the devastating criticisms of someone like Jerome McGann, who states bluntly that the "whole point" of a poem like this one is "to dissolve social and political conflicts in the mediations of art and beauty." It is also a response to how much Keats scholars love Keats, and how much it bothers them to see Shelley—the Oxford-educated son of a baronet—get the edge over their (sort of) working-class hero. In an ultimately unpersuasive counter-attack, Tom Paulin scans "To Autumn" for evidence of radical sympathies: the poem's poppies are really "redcoat soldiers," its crickets "a figure for members of the radical underground, preparing to winter out in readiness for the spring."[2] "It may seem controversial," Paulin writes, but Keats, in addition to being a top-notch shill for art and beauty, "was also capable of writing coded political poems"—it's not his fault that we have trouble seeing it.

This claim doesn't seem especially controversial to me, nor does it seem true. When Keats wanted to write in a way that was obviously political, he did: see *Isabella*, with what one contemporary critic called its "schoolboy vituperation of trade and traders," and Shaw its Marxism avant la lettre. What he excelled at was a poetics of negation that insistently vaporizes any endorsement of the way things are. His work is not coded, because a code is a riddle and, like all riddles, it is meant to be solved. A negation—an annulment of the possibility of forgiving anything about the reality we are forced to endure—is meant to linger and deepen. There is no solution to it: it is not a conundrum but the signature of a crisis. Its job is to make crisis available, if only partially, to sensation and thought.

On first pass, though, "To Autumn" seems far from negative. It seems, on the contrary, full of celebration, abundance, gravity, life. The watchword of the first stout stanza is fruit, which appears three times in eleven lines, as though wherever the poem turns it sees more of the same delicious thing.

(2) Paulin's term "soldiers" is misleading. To be clear, the security forces present at Peterloo were not members of any army. They were private subjects (England would have no professional police force until 1829) using force against fellow civilians with the blessing of the local government. For a thorough account of the Manchester Yeomanry and related groups, see Robert Poole, *Peterloo: The English Uprising* (Oxford: Oxford University Press, 2019).

Nothing here is not tumescent, and even if we wanted to roll out some blank truism about ripeness being the overture to rot we would still have to admit that, as it stands, Keats begins by obliging us to experience a totally real fullness. Unlike "Ode to Melancholy," which waxes proverbial about how near growth lies to decay, "To Autumn" begins by locking us into a scene of present-tense gratification. And unlike "Ode to Psyche," whose susurrating finale makes the noise of things as they disappear, the sibilance of this stanza—from "mists" to "cells"—is intrusively *loud*. It fills our ears and hijacks our awareness so that we too are over-brimmed, knowing, for a few moments, nothing but this language and its great impenitent grace.

"The concept of natural beauty rubs on a wound." That's Adorno, who associates this wound with the violence that the artwork "inflicts on nature" by presuming at once to represent and replace it. In "To Autumn" the insult is natural beauty itself, how it persists undeniably in a world of extreme and naked horror. If you wanted to push it, you could say that this thought is only available to Keats after Peterloo, as if, in the wake of that bloodbath, the mere fact of beauty becomes distasteful. Adorno says something similar elsewhere: "Even the blossoming tree lies the moment its bloom is seen without the shadow of terror . . . even the innocent 'How lovely!' becomes an excuse for an existence outrageously unlovely."

If this poem agreed it would be more like "Ode on a Grecian Urn," which recoils even as it admits to deriving pleasure from art whose prerequisite is human suffering. But "To Autumn" has even less of what, if we weren't talking about poetry, we might call an argument. For all its virtuosic show of ease, the ode is poised on a very short brink. This lends it a distinctly white-knuckled quality, which you might not notice unless you asked why this poem *needs* to be so good, what emergency is needling it behind the scenes, and what hyperbolic effort has been put in place to keep it—the emergency—there.

In this ode, perfection is not an achievement but a style, and it is essential to what Keats is trying to say: the problem with beauty is not that it is so fragile but that it is so durable. It is there and true even in an avalanche of shit and despair. To acknowledge that fully, as this poem does, is a profound act of self-mortification. Every impeccable turn of every line is bought by shame, which can never be allowed to leech through the language it has hounded into being, lest it accidentally impersonate an alibi or a justification. That we can be here—on this planet, in this time, confined by these exact habits of survival—and still find things to call beautiful and to love or to be unable to stop loving is indefensible. But we are here, and we do. "To Autumn" confesses it for us.

*

it is
possible even on the east coast
to find an isolated place for target practice
success
will depend mostly on your state of mind:
meditate, pray, make love, be prepared
at any time, to die

*

If you wanted to make "To Autumn" a poem about Peterloo, you might pay special attention to that word "conspiring." It means exactly what you think it means. It names the same seditious relation as the phrase "Cato Street Conspiracy," which is what the press called a plan hatched on February 22, 1820, to kill the prime minister and all the members of his cabinet. Like Keats's ode, the Cato Street Conspiracy is formed in the aftermath of Peterloo. It happens in the resting phase of the revolutionary event, in its lull or breather, and that, too, is what conspiring means: breathing together. "How lovely and doomed," writes Spahr, "this connection of everyone with lungs." Five of the conspirators were transported to Australia, and five were hung at Newgate Prison; two had testified against the others, and they went free. The five that were hung— Arthur Thistlewood, Richard Tidd, James Ings, William Davidson, and John Brunt—were decapitated postmortem. A contemporary account describes the scene:

> From the manner in which the last part of the execution was performed, very little blood was seen on the scaffold. The bodies being placed in a sitting attitude in their coffins, the blood could not flow copiously from them at the moment their heads were taken off. It was not till they were laid in an horizontal position, that the vital stream could escape freely from the heart.

The conspirators were executed in May, in the brisk English spring. Their conspiracy is not "To Autumn" and their blood is not its last oozings. But they belong to the same long, muddy season, where a break in the action allows at once for slackening and stealth, for the variously reluctant and rejuvenating encounter with beauty and the passionate confidences of treason.

The second stanza of "To Autumn" is about death. From the almost comical profusion of the first eleven lines, we move on to a heavily, almost laboriously symbolic tableau of mortality. Keats gives us "winnowing," he gives us "half-reap'd" and reaping's instrument, the scythe or "hook." He gives us the poppy (more opiate than redcoat) and in the cider-press and the look of patience cast upon it the hologram of a torture device, since to be patient, after all, is not just to wait but to suffer. If the downtime of insurrection is sometimes quiet—and this stanza is seriously lulled or "drows'd"—it is nonetheless replete with effort, much of it painful. Some survive and some don't; some are cut down and others spared. This whole stanza is built around an image of old-fashioned agricultural labor but there is something massive and relentless about it, and something mechanical, too. As the pristine iambs of the first five lines slow to a grind over "Drows'd" and "Spares," while the staccato taps of "Steady" shiver and jerk, the artwork is at risk of becoming an appliance.

If Autumn is not a machine, it has the indifference of one, "sitting careless," unconcerned by the microscopic drama of who lives and who dies, who manages to accept, somehow, our terrible confluence of good and evil, and who simply can't, not because such a person is weak or intemperate but because this is the math of half-reaping: roughly 50 percent won't survive, whatever survival means. It's to Autumn that Keats speaks the reassuring phrase, "Think not of them, thou hast thy music too," but what if it weren't? Or rather, what if he meant to address not the season but the way of life for which it stands: the interim between riot and revolution we might be tempted to call, with our enemies, the time of our defeat?

There is a way to read the ode as a celebration of passivity. Autumn changes dress from the first to second stanza, goes from being the architect of abundance—loading, blessing, bending, filling, swelling, plumping, budding—to a sleepy, even drugged-out figure of resignation. This Autumn stands (or dozes) at a good distance from what Keats calls its music, which, by the third stanza, has been outsourced to birds, lambs, bugs. Autumn's music, in other words, is less *in* Autumn than *around* it. That music also echoes the fatalism of the poem's velvet middle: the mourning of the gnats is linked to the arbitrary movement of the wind, which buffets their tiny bodies as it lives or dies. These gnats, too, are half-reaped, as powerless to choose whether to live or die, fly or fall as the robin is to refuse to whistle or the cricket to rasp its wings.

The gambit of Shelley's "Mask of Anarchy" is that passivity is the best form of resistance. It is so potent that it doesn't even need human beings, just their blood: slaughter talks, "eloquent, oracular." To write that poem, Shelley relied on newspaper accounts of Peterloo and mainly on those published in the *Examiner*, the weekly run by his and Keats's friend Leigh Hunt. The *Examiner* is often referred to as a radical publication but that's not quite true; by the late eighteen-teens it had nestled into a cozy centrism that would later prompt William Hazlitt to write that "political, is like military warfare. There are but two sides, and after you have once chosen your party, it will not do to stand in the midway, and say you like neither."

And so it is not surprising that the *Examiner* leaned heavily on the report of a sympathetic "Manchester gentleman" to insist on the total vulnerability of the Peterloo crowd and its nonaggression even when under attack. As this anonymous witness put it, "the Yeomen had literally to cut and hack a road" across the field, "and this they did through a people *absolutely passive*—no *resistance of any kind* was, or indeed could be offered." Reports that "stones were thrown &c" are, he hastened to add, "*altogether false.*"

"The Mask of Anarchy" approves and so does Shelley, whose commitment to nonviolence is arguably the most significant political feature of his work. Remember what Hope says: "What they like, that let them do." But that is not the whole story of Peterloo, which in no way proves that nonviolence has a moral monopoly on resistance. Here's more from Bamford's *Passages*:

A heroine, a young married woman of our party, with her face all bloody, her hair streaming about her, her bonnet hanging by the string, and her apron weighted with stones, kept her assailant at bay until she fell backwards and was near being taken; but she got away covered with severe bruises. It was near this place and about this time that one of the Yeomanry was dangerously wounded, and unhorsed, by a blow from the fragment of a brick; and it was supposed to have been flung by this woman.

Bamford's memoirs weren't published for another twenty-five years, but after Peterloo it quickly emerged that several members of the Yeomanry and other security personnel were hit, and hit hard, with sticks and stones by what one protestor, a man named William Buckley, called a "people determined to resist." One had his ear halfway cut off by a brickbat. To dismiss these reports, as historians often have, by painting Peterloo's victims as helpless or placid is an understandable but misguided impulse. Whatever compelling ethical claims exist for nonviolence, it has never been the only response to state terrorism. If we pretend that it is, then those who choose to resist differently—like Bamford's young heroine—appear disposable, the harm that comes to them justified. With all due respect to Shelley, it's hard to read "The Mask of Anarchy" and not conclude that the only good dissident is a dead one.

*

but don't get uptight: the guns
will not win this one, they are
an incidental part of the action
which we better damn well be good at,
what will win

is mantras, the sustenance we give each other,
the energy we plug into
   (the fact that we touch
    share food)
the buddha nature
of everyone, friend or foe, like a million earthworms
tunneling under this structure
till it falls

        *

Diane di Prima's "Revolutionary Letter #7" gives hope to
Keats's ode. This doesn't let "To Autumn" off the hook, and
besides the poem wouldn't want that. What it wants is to show
us the human incapacity for resisting beauty—to show us that
it really is impossible sometimes not to love the world, even
when it provides ample evidence that it should not be loved.
Keats does his best to present this state of affairs in a way that
is neutral and detached. He refuses to make excuses for the
poem, to discharge its difficult energies in the vapid, hysterical
idiom of "complicity." Instead, he forces us to inhabit an ex-
cruciating contradiction: we are attached, despite everything,
to this place that has been weaponized against us, where the
earth ingests our oozings and its ambient noises muffle our
screams. We are attached, too, to poems about this place, es-
pecially when they commute suffering to metaphor—a half-
reaped furrow, a choir of ululating bugs.

  Di Prima pulls up to this contradiction and calmly exter-
minates it. She begins with an appeal to those not necessarily
in the know—to those, perhaps, more comfortable with odes
than with Molotov cocktails, flamethrowers, bombs, "what-
ever" might be needed for what she calls "the action." This is
a euphemism and it is also not. Like conspiracy, "the action"

does not rise to the high status of an event; it is anonymous, collective, and extempore, a name for a concrete but open-ended intensity to which some unidentified people are giving everything they have for an unspecified amount of time. Think about how we might use those words in everyday speech, to describe a happening of whose nature and contours and content we are basically ignorant: *I'm going where the action is,* in search of an undisclosed excitement. The action is between phenomenon and wish. It is also a sort of code word, the part of the story where a bomb might drop, a rock might fly, an assassin get knocked off his horse, but you wouldn't want to say so out loud, not in certain company.

Why the East Coast? Unlike California or the Midwest, the East Coast is densely populated, built-up; this is the backdrop of di Prima's reassurance that *even* there it's possible to find a place to shoot a gun. But the East Coast, with its varicella rash of universities hugging the shoreline, is also a Green Zone of sophistication and prestige, the kind of place where someone might dutifully suggest that reports of stones thrown at Peterloo's precursory cops are suspect if they come from Tory sources.

"Success" in such a context would mean not only finding a place for target practice, nor only the success of an ongoing struggle that occasionally and unpredictably coils into *the action*. It would also mean silencing a pedantic chorus of scruples, turning instead to the mind-emptying practices of meditation, prayer, sex, and provisioning for death. Keats would appreciate this spin on "buddha nature," which—as di Prima suggests—means compassion for all living things but also a divestment from any beliefs or attitudes motivated by ego. In di Prima's poem, Buddha nature has the same inborn voluptuousness as Negative Capability: it is discovered in touch and eating together, in shared knowledge and brusque encouragement ("don't get uptight").

Here is how di Prima inches past Keats, as far as loving the world goes. Whereas Keats makes us sit in the discomfort of our own receptivity to beauty—the beauty of nature and of his poem—di Prima reminds us that we have to live for something and then orders us to do it, and to do it with each other. His ode to Autumn is a snapshot of one unacceptable aspect of an unacceptable existence, her letter an intimation of its fall. Fall, or rather "falls," is the last word of di Prima's poem, which promises that a consciousness freed from simple antagonism—friend and foe, gun and mantra—can turn impasse into action, loosening and ultimately leveling "this structure" of one thing versus another.

But that's not all "this structure" is. This structure is this poem, and as long as it is not a gun, not sex, not a mantra, and not a million earthworms it also has a bomb coming to it. Di Prima's language is not Keats's (how could it be?), but they are making the same promise: to hold so tight onto poetry it surrenders its shape, to hold so tight onto us that we do, too.

Sources

Theodor Adorno. *Aesthetic Theory*. Edited and translated by Robert Hullot-Kentor. Minneapolis: University of Minnesota Press, 1998.

———. *Minima Moralia: Reflections on Damaged Life*. London: Verso, 2006.

Samuel Bamford [with Jemima Bamford]. *Passages in the Life of a Radical*. London: Simpkin, Marshall, 1844.

Diane di Prima. "Revolutionary Letter #7." In *Revolutionary Letters*. San Francisco: City Lights Books, 1971.

The *Examiner*. 12 September 1819.

William Hazlitt. "On the Spirit of Partisanship." In *The Complete Works of William Hazlitt*, vol. 17, edited by P. P. Howe. 21 vols. London: J. M. Dent & Sons, 1930–34.

Jerome J. McGann. *The Romantic Ideology: A Critical Investigation*. Chicago: University of Chicago Press, 1983.

Tom Paulin. *The Secret Life of Poems: A Poetry Primer*. New York: Faber and Faber, 2011.

Robert Poole. *Peterloo: The English Uprising*. Oxford: Oxford University Press, 2019.

Juliana Spahr. "It's All Good, It's All Fucked." In *That Winter the Wolf Came*. Oakland: Commune Editions, 2015.

———. *This Connection of Everyone with Lungs*. Berkeley: University of California Press, 2005.

The Trials of Arthur Thistlewood and Others for High Treason: At the Old Bailey Sessions-House, Commencing on Saturday the 15th and Ending on Thursday the 27th of April 1820. London: Sherwood, Neeley, & Johns, 1820.

Postscript: Sleep and Poetry

I introduced this book as a work of criticism that is also a love story, and it is: my kind of love story, the record of an attempt to see something clearly, to pay the best attention to it I can. As I wrote I often wished for the authority of another kind of love—the imperious poetical kind, which doesn't hesitate to tell the object exactly what it means. This book would be different if I knew how to love like that. The truth is, there is no voice I don't hear louder than my own.

Somewhere Keats calls poetry a higher form of sleep—a dream that interrupts the world. In my own higher sleep I dreamt that I draped myself across your back, but you stood up suddenly and I was knocked to the ground. I dreamt I was trapped on a bus with you while it was snowing and you seemed unbelievably young. I dreamt of a room filled with lamps. I dreamt you kept taking my hand even though I didn't want us to be seen together, and later you laid your head down on my knee. I dreamt I got stuck in a yellow locker but it occurred to me I could use my weight to tip it over and kick free so I did. I consciously told myself that when I was with you I could also do this. I didn't dream about you but around 5:00 a.m. I heard a voice scream your full name, and I was wrenched off the bed as though someone were pulling me by the hair.

I dreamt of a rash on your arms and a plan I made to care for it. I dreamt I woke up in the same bed as you, and that it was unbearable. I dreamt we spent the afternoon together and ran down to the beach. We were laughing and playing, then you picked me up by the elbows and flung me out to sea, where I began to sink. I swam hard and was able to crawl onto the shore, tiny pink shells biting my cheek. You started to come toward me and I braced myself to do it again. It wouldn't have been right to call it attraction. I wanted to put my body between you and the world, that's all. In a long wait for the last war I had been waiting also for you.

Acknowledgments

Many thanks to everyone at the University of Chicago Press—in particular Carrie Olivia Adams, Jenni Fry, Meredith Nini, Randy Petilos, and Alan Thomas—for being so supportive of this project, and to Nicholas Murray for his exceptionally sensitive editing.

Each of these pages holds the thread of a conversation with a friend without whom they wouldn't have been written. I am happily obliged to Lauren Berlant, Fred D'Aguiar, Nan Z. Da, Zoe Kazan, Anthony Madrid, Maureen McLane, Dandi Meng, Michael Robbins, Juliana Spahr, and Jesslyn Whittell, either for reading the manuscript as it was coming together or for talking me out of doing other things so I could do this instead.

Tatianna Morales knew the book was there before I did. It is dedicated to her, with gratitude.

Index